JB JOSSEY-BASS™
A Wiley Brand

Attention-Grabbing Events

Nonprofit Events That Draw Interest and Support to Your Cause

Scott C. Stevenson, Editor

WILEY

Attention-Grabbing Events:
Nonprofit Events That
Draw Interest and Support to Your Cause

Published by

Stevenson, Inc.
P.O. Box 4528 • Sioux City, Iowa • 51104
Phone 712.239.3010 • Fax 712.239.2166
www.stevensoninc.com

TABLE OF CONTENTS

Chapter 1: **Announcements, Press Releases and Promotional Strategies** 4
- *Five Ways to Maximize Major Event Publicity*
- *Get Creative When Seeking Pre-event Publicity*
- *Announce a New Gift As You Go Public With Capital Campaign*
- *Unique Ways to Publicize Your Organization's Achievements*
- *Opera Celebrates Golden Anniversary By Giving Back*
- *Marketing Seminar Benefits Whole Community*

Chapter 2: **Leveraging Anniversaries and Milestones** 7
- *10 Ideas to Host Successful Grand Reopening Event*
- *Celebrating 50 Years*
- *Anniversary Inspires Yearlong Celebration, Multitude of Special Events*
- *Identify Reunion Occasions*
- *Anniversary Lends Itself to Celebrating, Wooing Major Donors*
- *Diamond Theme Inspires 75th Anniversary Celebrations*
- *Celebrate Anniversary of Building Dedication*

Chapter 3: **Awards and Appreciation Events** 11
- *Appreciation-themed Events Build Goodwill, Publicity*
- *Use Employee Retirement to Highlight Your Organization*
- *Honor Top Supporters With a Recognition Award*
- *University Hosts Leaders in Management Award Dinner*
- *Awards Ceremony Honors Heroes of All Breeds*
- *Make 'Philanthropist of the Year' Award a Special Occasion*
- *Organization Combines Donor, Volunteer Recognition Events*
- *Honor Retiring CEO With Memorable Celebration*
- *Recognize Top Mentors*
- *Award Encourages Faculty Fundraising*

Chapter 4: **Programs and Experiences That Make an Impact** 16
- *'Day in the District' Shows Local Leaders a Day in the Life*
- *Craft Bar Bonds Membership Community*
- *Engage Supporters, Community With "Name Our Mascot' Contest*
- *Tribute Tree Program Roots College in Its Past*
- *Weekly Winter Program Series Helps Reach Broader Audience*
- *Solar Workshop Shines Spotlight on School*
- *Attract Current and Prospective Members With a Trunk Show*
- *Program Club Boosts Good Will and Giving*
- *Pampering Event Promotes Wellness, Local Business*

Chapter 5: **Utilizing Celebrities and Speakers** 21
- *To Get Celebrities to Your Event, Challenge Them*
- *Donors Support Professionals With Endowed Lecture Series*
- *Create a Speakers' Bureau to Promote Membership, Members*
- *Organization's Theme Ties In to Event — Supporting Literacy*
- *Invite Celebrities to Speak at Your Member Breakfasts*
- *Make Your Star-studded Event a Success*

Chapter 6: **Construction and Dedication Events** 25
- *Ground-breaking Ceremonies Highlight Donors, Spark Interest*
- *Host Grand Openings With Local Flair*
- *Share Construction Updates With Donors, Would-be Donors*
- *Mark Construction Milestone With Topping-off Ceremony*
- *Host a Dedication Event That Attendees Won't Forget*

TABLE OF CONTENTS

Chapter 7:   **Engaging Tours and Open Houses** 28

- *Keep Your Open House Relevant*
- *Give Tours That Invite Support*
- *Educate, Entertain Visitors With VIP Tours*
- *Tours Get Major Donors Passionate About Your Cause*
- *Engaging Guests Fosters Tour Participation*
- *Holiday Open House Combines Member, Volunteer Recognition*
- *Plan a Tour-of-corporate-offices Event*
- *Valentine Membership Party Opens Doors of Opportunity*

Chapter 8:   **Reaching Out Through Volunteer-focused Events** 32

- *Combine Volunteer Appreciation With Education*
- *Wednesday Night Work Nights Draw Dedicated Volunteers*
- *Appreciation Event Celebrates Volunteer Accomplishments*
- *Volunteer-assisted Story Project Strengthens Organization*
- *Luncheon Series Provides Boost for Volunteerism*
- *Hold Raffle to Fund Volunteer Recognition*
- *Annual Garden Celebration Features Volunteer Display*

Chapter 9:   **Notable Fundraisers and Friend-raisers** 36

- *Celebrate the Unusual for Unforgettable Fundraising Festivals*
- *Chasing Ambulances Helps Victims of Violence*
- *White Coat Day Gets to the Heart of Fundraising*
- *Involve Younger Constituents At a Summer Beach Party*
- *Scrapbookers Raise Funds to Battle Cancer*
- *Adult Spelling Bee Generates Media Exposure*
- *Book-themed Fundraiser Writes a Success Story for Library*
- *Scrabble® Challenge Tests Skill, Raises Big Bucks*
- *Puzzle-filled Event Builds Excitement, Raises Funds*
- *Casting for a Cure Offers New Twist for Fishing Tourneys*
- *Motorcycle Riders Cruise to Victory in Fundraising Efforts*
- *Branding, Varied Activities Ensure a Dazzling Event*
- *Groups Carve Creative Path in Race to Raise Funds, Awareness*
- *Signed, Sealed & Delivered — Original Art by Mystery Artisans*

Chapter 10:   **Keys to Creating Top-notch Events** 44

- *Host Receptions to Die for*
- *Pre-event Supports Nonprofit's Ongoing Efforts*
- *Make Humor the Center Attraction for Your Special Event*
- *Organize and Host Effective Rummage Sales*
- *Engage Young Audience With Texting Contest*
- *Snag a Celebrity Chef to Raise the Bar at Your Next Special Event*
- *First Annual Event Puts the 'Fun' in Fun Day*
- *Checklist Helps Organize Show-stopping Open House*
- *Enliven Celebrations With Talent Competitions*

Chapter 11:   **Online, Virtual and Electronic Tools** 49

- *Twitter-driven Event Draws Crowd in 15 Days*
- *Fundraising Video Connects Supporters to Their Cause*
- *Encourage Current, Potential Members With Online Video Tour*
- *Virtual Walkers Extend Event Reach*
- *Photo Tour Showcases New Addition*
- *Photo Contest Engages Constituents, Introduces New Mascot*
- *Twitter-based Fundraiser Brings in $10,000 in 10 Days*

Attention-Grabbing Events: Nonprofit Events That Draw Interest and Support to Your Cause

ANNOUNCEMENTS, PRESS RELEASES AND PROMOTIONAL STRATEGIES

Whether your organization has just secured a major donation, launched an exciting new program or staged a high-profile gathering, you want people to know! Effectively publicizing your successes — and promoting the details of upcoming events and activities — is a key component of building awareness of your organization and its work.

Five Ways to Maximize Major Event Publicity

Some special events impact your organization beyond a mere press release, and you hope to maximize the positive attention they bring. Develop a variety of ways to share the news with different audiences, but in different ways.

1. **Share client testimonials**. Your organization has been named top provider of services in your field by an independent group. Ask some of the most compelling clients you have served to go on camera or on the record for commercials, advertisements and feature stories that you can use at intervals throughout the year.

2. **Spotlight your benefactors**. A longtime supporter has left your institution a bequest that will allow you to build an addition, or ensures continuity of services for years to come. Who is or was this person? Write an article about his or her life, association with your organization and reasons for choosing you for this major gift. Explain how it will positively impact the community.

3. **Publicize first-in-the-region status**. Being first to obtain life-saving equipment, whether at the fire station or in the operating room, is a claim to fame you can enjoy even after competitors have caught up. Develop a brief but descriptive tagline to use on all publications and advertising for as long as applicable, or until you have a new first to promote.

4. **Host a celebration activity**. Invite the community to share in your good fortune by holding an open house, family festival or free concert that trumpets your good news while also showing your gratitude. Publicity for the event should center on the reason for the celebration and result in free media coverage.

5. **Award a scholarship**. Helping a deserving student who has a connection to your organization is an excellent way to express thanks for community support that led to your achievement. Media coverage about the recipient also will bounce back to the reason you founded the scholarship in the first place.

Get Creative When Seeking Pre-event Publicity

Press releases and media interviews are excellent ways to attract publicity before your special event, but you may need to do more than that to truly grab the spotlight and inspire audiences to attend.

As appropriate, add these elements to your publicity repertoire:

❑ Announce changes and additions. Has the sluggish economy caused you to rethink your target audience? Tell the press. If your formal gala is now a festive family celebration with reduced ticket or table prices, that's a human interest story. Be upbeat about providing better value for your supporters and drawing a potentially larger audience.

❑ Arrange interviews with honorees. Create a buzz around the people you are honoring at your event. Tell the public why they are worthy of recognition from the entire community. Even those who cannot attend will be more aware of your organization's mission and services, and admire those who help make it successful.

❑ Invite the public to watch the event. While most people buy tickets to help you reach your goal, look for opportunities or activities spectators can observe free of charge. For example, a competition to hit a hole in one or shoot a basket for a large cash prize or a fireworks show can generate advance media coverage and community interest.

❑ Start a fun awareness campaign. A first step might be a billboard or newspaper ad announcing only "It's coming." Add details once a week like "It's coming August 8th" and "It's coming August 8th to Community Hospital" until the who, what, when, where and why are fully revealed.

❑ Offer free admission to the first 10 (or other such number) people. A famous author is donating and signing books for you. A popular rock band is giving a benefit concert and selling CDs. All signs point to a sellout, but you can generate good will and positive publicity by giving away a few spots to early birds who are fans of your event's star.

ANNOUNCEMENTS, PRESS RELEASES AND PROMOTIONAL STRATEGIES

Announce a New Gift As You Go Public With Capital Campaign

In fundraising, as in comedy, timing is everything.

Timing is especially important when announcing a major campaign — you want donors to hear about your campaign at a time when a) they are excited to give, and b) they feel their donation will make the greatest impact.

For these reasons, the timing was perfect for officials at the Saint Louis Zoo, who recently announced the public phase of their $120 million campaign under the best of circumstances. Not only were they able to announce making well over half of their goal during the private phase of their campaign, they also announced a handful of record-breaking major gifts, all on the 100th anniversary of the zoo's opening in 1910.

"We don't have elaborate events all the time," explains Cynthia Holter, director of external relations, referring to the large centennial gala her team put together, "It all sort of culminated." Holter explains that her team launched the $120 million campaign's quiet phase in 2007, and had hoped to be ready to announce it by the centennial celebration. Then, when the $5 million gift came in, the donor requested the announcement be saved for the celebration as well.

"We wanted a chance to honor the guests in a really special way," she says, "not just the $5 million gift, but also a $1 million corporate gift, and a $3 million bequest, as well as the many donors that came out of the woodwork to support the zoo in time for the event. It was huge for us."

The event itself was a major production complete with Grammy award-winning music and fireworks. Holter made sure that donors at all levels were invited.

"For these events," she says, "we've found the more the merrier. Even those who haven't given large gifts are worthy of being recognized. And as we talk to people about

---

Minicampaigns: Mobilize Donations Around Event Deadlines

Planning a major non-fundraising event? You can still use the opportunity to encourage immediate giving.

Cynthia Holter, director of external relations at the Saint Louis Zoo (St. Louis, MO), shares how her organization's centennial anniversary celebration allowed her to mobilize donors who had been waiting to give:

"We used the event as a sort of deadline, letting people know that we would be including donor names in the program for this major event, and if they wanted to recognized at that time, they could give before June 3."

The effort inspired 25 donors to give between the announcement and deadline, including four major bequests valued at $7.5 million, $1.3 million, $725,000 and $389,000.

---

bequests, we let them know they can turn some of those bequests into cash gifts for more recognition opportunities. We want people to think, 'I have the zoo in my estate plan, I should tell them.'"

The event was a success. Holter received 30 e-mails and numerous calls from donors the next morning, thanking her for a lovely time and a great evening; she even heard from several new donors. "The event and the announcement got people talking," Holter says. "It was very much worth it."

Source: Cynthia Holter, Director of External Relations, Saint Louis Zoo, St. Louis, MO. Phone (314) 646-4691.
E-mail: holter@stlzoo.org. Website: www.stlzoo.org

Unique Ways to Publicize Your Organization's Achievements

Being first, coming in last or building a better service program are all worthy occasions for tooting your organization's horn. Go beyond the usual press releases and television appearances to publicize your accomplishment with a new twist.

Consider:

✓ **Creating an iconic character/spokesperson.** Imagine your ideal ambassador. If the story of The Princess and the Pea could describe the launch of your new sleeping disorders clinic, audition local talent for the role of the center's face and voice for personal and media appearances.

✓ **Visually illustrating your accomplishment.** The more creative or unusual your display, the greater the media interest. If your hospital ranked first in outcomes for a cardiac procedure, build a giant model of a human heart with playground features like slides and tunnels for children to explore. Or if your community pantry served

its 3,000th Thanksgiving meal, hold an open house serving 3,000 pumpkin bars or cookies to visitors.

✓ **Hosting a workshop or lesson tied to your accomplishment.** Now that your organization has positioned itself as a leader in a specific area, share that knowledge with a public seminar on a topic in that arena. If your college was the first wireless campus in the state, have your technology students do an internet tutorial on how to set up your own network at home in easy-to-follow steps.

✓ **Using business journals to your advantage.** These more highly focused publications allow you to feature the more technical aspects of your organization's achievements than would a general interest story in your newspaper's business section. They also lend themselves to interviews with those persons who were directly responsible for the accomplishment.

ANNOUNCEMENTS, PRESS RELEASES AND PROMOTIONAL STRATEGIES

Opera Celebrates Golden Anniversary By Giving Back

Vancouver Opera (Vancouver, BC) is celebrating its golden anniversary by giving back to the communities that have supported it for the past 50 years.

In partnership with the staff of Vancouver-based resource leader Goldcorp, Inc. — which made a major gift to the opera through a three-year sponsorship — the opera's artists, staff, volunteers, supporters and board members will provide 10,000 hours of volunteer service to various charities from July 1, 2009 to June 30, 2010 through the opera's Community Connections volunteer service program.

In the first month of the program alone, they already banked more than 1,500 hours, says Christopher Libby, the opera's managing director.

"The Vancouver Opera Board and staff thought that giving back to the community was a great way to demonstrate our thanks for 50 years of support," Libby says. "Everybody throws a gala for their anniversary (as we will), and we thought this was a great way to demonstrate that the opera and its fans contribute back to the community in a myriad of ways outside the opera house."

Through the effort, Libby says they hope to support other local charities while showcasing the opera's offstage contributions to the community, fostering new relationships between opera supporters and local charities and inspiring others to do likewise.

Opera representatives approached Goldcorp about the sponsorship gift through a member of the opera's board, Steven Dean, who arranged the initial meeting with Goldcorp leadership. Libby says they chose Goldcorp because of its long history of community engagement in the areas it operates.

"Mr. Dean offered to make a contact as a fellow mining industry executive," he says. "Plus, we thought our golden anniversary might have special appeal to them (because of the company name). Mr. Dean went to the extra effort to arrange his attendance via cell phone despite being on a mining trip to Argentina at the time of the meeting."

Libby and staff are getting the word out about the program through press releases, e-mail blasts, its web page (www.vancouveropera.ca), its blog (http://vancouveropera.blogspot.com/), Twitter(www.twitter.com/VancouverOpera), Facebook (www.facebook.com/vancouveropera), YouTube(www.youtube.com/user/vancouveropera) and promotions through the charities supported by the effort.

Source: Christopher Libby, Managing Director, Vancouver Opera, Vancouver, British Columbia, Canada. Phone (604) 331-4824. E-mail: clibby@vancouveropera.ca

Marketing Seminar Benefits Whole Community

What does your nonprofit do exceptionally well? Always be on the lookout for ways to share that information in a positive light.

John DeCelle, chief marketing officer for the nonprofit credit union, SEFCU (Albany, NY), says the credit union's purpose is "to help our members achieve their dreams and make our communities better places to live."

In 2009 alone, DeCelle says, "We supported 350 nonprofits in our regions, donating $1.8 million, and volunteering at their events. As a result, we are often called upon to assist with the marketing needs of those organizations. So our president and CEO, Michael Castellana, suggested it would be a great idea to provide a marketing seminar."

The seminar, designed to provide nonprofits with marketing knowledge they might not have at their fingertips, had local media experts discussing how to develop marketing plans, put together a media buy, work with the media to tell the organization's story and utilize social media to its fullest advantage. There was no cost to attend.

DeCelle says they received such positive feedback regarding the seminar that they are developing a follow-up seminar.

"Attendees benefited by having free access to professionals that they would not have had otherwise," he says. "Providing marketing expertise to nonprofits enhances their ability to communicate to their various audiences, ultimately benefiting the entire community."

Source: John DeCelle, Chief Marketing Officer, SEFCU, Albany, NY. Phone (518) 464-5243. E-mail: jdecelle@sefcu.com

Attention-Grabbing Events: Nonprofit Events That Draw Interest and Support to Your Cause

LEVERAGING ANNIVERSARIES AND MILESTONES

Anniversaries present a unique occasion to look back over victories won and accomplishments achieved. Whether your organization is approaching a fifth anniversary or a 50th, seize the opportunity to tell the world not only where you've been, but where you are going — with their support, of course.

10 Ideas to Host Successful Grand Reopening Event

If your organization is preparing to unveil new benefits, new giving level structures, a new location or new logo, make the most of this news by hosting a grand reopening.

Here are 10 ideas to get the most mileage out of your significant addition or change while celebrating current supporters and encouraging others to join:

1. Choose what type of event will work best for your organization and your community: An open house? A casual picnic? A formal dinner? A community educational forum?

2. Consider offering two or more times for the event to allow guests a casual daytime option with light luncheon fare and a business-attire evening event complete with a social hour, appetizers and cocktails.

3. Invite all guests from your organization's original opening, all current supporters, lapsed supporters, city/county/state officials, the news media and new members of the community.

4. Offer reporters a behind-the-scenes tour or other exclusive access a few days before the event to generate publicity — and traffic — on your big day.

5. Create a business-to-business grand reopening offering special discounts or trial memberships to other business professionals in your community.

6. Work with organizations aligned with your goals to showcase all resources and organizations in your region.

7. Ask local notables to speak on behalf of your organization. Include long-standing supporters, especially those well known in your community, to share their experiences by way of a short presentation during the event.

8. Prominently feature the new aspects of your organization. Have on hand new brochures and fact sheets that highlight what's new about your organization and provide details about your donor base.

9. Offer a trial membership with an expiration date to get more potential new members crossing your threshold.

10. Always have staff on hand to answer questions about your new offerings and enroll members.

Celebrating 50 Years

To celebrate 50 years in the field of scientific research, the Children's Hospital Oakland Research Institute (CHORI) of Oakland, CA, hosted a gala in October 2009 at the Chabot Space & Science Center (Oakland, CA). Jessika Diamond, interim special events manager, answers questions about the crowd-pleasing event:

Why was the venue of the Chabot Space & Science Center chosen for the event?

"Holding our party in a venue dedicated to science and education was a natural fit. The event began with scientific talks, furthering the theme."

What was unique about the gala?

"Our event was interactive — the reception took place just outside the Beyond Blastoff: Surviving in Space exhibit and we have pictures of guests trying out the interactive exhibits. They enjoyed defying gravity or pretending to be a shuttle repair crew member, and it added to the fun of the location, which added to the meaning of the event."

How else did you celebrating 50 years?

"We held a symposium in March 2010 at CHORI, featuring luminaries in related fields, including genetics, immunobiol-ogy, cancer and more discussing the latest discoveries and trends in their fields. Since no celebration of the past and present is complete without looking forward, we included talks and poster presentations from the young researchers at CHORI, the fellows and post-docs."

What tips can you share for marking a significant milestone at an organization?

"Use a milestone anniversary as an opportunity for a fundraising campaign.... Also, use this opportunity to blow your organization's horn about what's been accomplished over time. Use photos, retrospectives, histories and other ways that really promote why the organization has survived those five decades. Discussions of alumni, successes, achievements are also pertinent. You're essentially throwing a birthday party, and what birthday party doesn't focus on how wonderful the birthday boy or girl is?"

Source: Jessika Diamond, Special Events Manager (Interim), Children's Hospital & Research Center Foundation, Oakland, CA. Phone (510) 428-3885. E-mail: Jdiamond@mail.cho.org. Website: www.childrenshospitaloakland.org

LEVERAGING ANNIVERSARIES AND MILESTONES

Anniversary Inspires Yearlong Celebration, Multitude of Special Events

If your organization is gearing up for a major anniversary celebration, consider hosting a series of events equal to the number of years you are celebrating.

The year 2009 marked the 50th anniversary of the Natural Resources Council of Maine (NRCM) of Augusta, ME. To mark the occasion, staff and volunteers organized 50 events to celebrate their 50 years of work protecting Maine's environment.

"We decided a drumbeat of events was the best way to keep our anniversary celebration on the radar screen for our members and to engage the broader public," says Allison Wells, senior director, public affairs and marketing.

Planners came up with the concept several years prior and started planning for the 50 events in 2008. They began with monthly meetings for key staff and board members and increased to every two weeks when 2009 approached. A committee of five people focused on the celebration, including other staff members as needed.

Rather than create 50 brand new events, the committee reviewed the council's existing schedule of yearly events to discuss ways in which they could add a 50th anniversary message to each.

"We flagged certain kinds of events as necessary. Then we set up a spreadsheet of categories like 'Indoors,' 'Outdoors,' 'Staff-led,' 'Self-guided' and also flagged ways to tie activities to nationally or state-recognized special awareness days and weeks," says Wells. "We brought this to an all-staff brainstorm session and made sure we included a wide range of activities, from informal brown-bag lectures to more formal events. We were very careful to make sure we included things that were just plain fun but that fit with our mission and our goals for the celebration.

"Then the real work began, which included sketching out a timeline and assigning staff in various roles."

Organizers also tapped in to events being hosted by other groups that made sense for the organization to be affiliated with and that would garner significant attention.

"For example, we worked with Bates College (Lewiston, ME) to locate an appropriate speaker for the college's prestigious Edmund S. Muskie lecture," she says. "Our executive director introduced the speaker and both groups promoted the event."

Source: Allison Wells, Senior Director, Public Affairs and Marketing, Natural Resources Council of Maine, Augusta, ME. Phone (207) 622-3101, ext. 280. E-mail: awells@nrcm.org

This 50-year timeline, featured in the Winter 2009 newsletter for the Natural Resources Council of Maine (Augusta, ME) marks significant events in its five-decade history.

Multi-faceted Promotions Buoy Yearlong Celebration

To promote a year-long celebration of 50 events to mark the 50th anniversary for the National Resources Council of Maine (NRCM) of Augusta, ME, staff chose a multi-faceted approach.

They included an anniversary tagline on letterhead and constantly updated their website to showcase upcoming events related to the celebration. They also used their quarterly newsletter to showcase the accomplishments of the last 50 years with a time line (see below), promoted anniversary events and celebrated members who took part in the activities.

NRCM staff use online social networking sites such as Facebook and Twitter to get the word out, too.

"We were fortunate to have skilled and creative staff to plan and execute the ideas, which eliminated the need to hire consultants and outside communication firms," noted Allison Wells, senior director, public affairs and marketing.

To encourage people to stay enthusiastic and engaged throughout the year, organizers hosted a raffle for outdoor-related prizes (e.g., kayaks, canoes and lobster bakes). Persons who attend an anniversary event or participated in a self-scheduled event earned points that translated into entry in the raffle.

For more on the yearlong celebration, visit: www.nrcm.org/50_years.asp

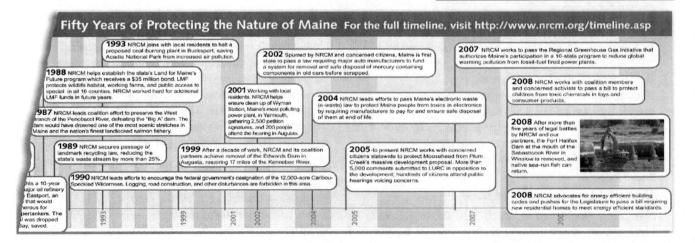

Fifty Years of Protecting the Nature of Maine For the full timeline, visit http://www.nrcm.org/timeline.asp

1993 NRCM joins with local residents to halt a proposed coal-burning plant in Bucksport, saving Acadia National Park from increased air pollution.

2002 Spurred by NRCM and concerned citizens, Maine is first state to pass a law requiring major auto manufacturers to fund a system for removal and safe disposal of mercury containing components in old cars before scrapped.

2007 NRCM works to pass the Regional Greenhouse Gas Initiative that authorizes Maine's participation in a 10-state program to reduce global warming pollution from fossil-fuel fired power plants.

1988 NRCM helps establish the state's Land for Maine's Future program which receives a $35 million bond. LMF protects wildlife habitat, working farms, and public access to special in all 16 counties. NRCM worked hard for additional LMF funds in future years.

2001 Working with local residents, NRCM helps ensure clean up of Wyman Station, Maine's most polluting power plant, in Yarmouth, gathering 2,500 petition signatures, and 200 people attend the hearing in Augusta.

2004 NRCM leads efforts to pass Maine's electronic waste (e-waste) law to protect Maine people from toxics in electronics by requiring manufacturers to pay for and ensure safe disposal of them at end of life.

2008 NRCM works with coalition members and concerned activists to pass a bill to protect children from toxic chemicals in toys and consumer products.

1987 NRCM leads coalition effort to preserve the West Branch of the Penobscot River, defeating the "Big A" dam. The dam would have drowned one of the most scenic stretches in Maine and the nation's finest landlocked salmon fishery.

2008 After more than five years of legal battles by NRCM and our partners, the Fort Halifax Dam at the mouth of the Sebasticook River in Winslow is removed, and native sea-run fish can return.

1989 NRCM secures passage of landmark recycling law, reducing the state's waste stream by more than 25%.

1999 After a decade of work, NRCM and its coalition partners achieve removal of the Edwards Dam in Augusta, restoring 17 miles of the Kennebec River.

2005-to present NRCM works with concerned citizens statewide to protect Moosehead from Plum Creek's massive development proposal. More than 5,000 comments submitted to LURC in opposition to the development; hundreds of citizens attend public hearings voicing concerns.

1990 NRCM leads efforts to encourage the federal government's designation of the 12,000-acre Caribou-Speckled Wilderness. Logging, road construction, and other disturbances are forbidden in this area.

2008 NRCM advocates for energy efficient building codes and pushes for the Legislature to pass a bill requiring new residential homes to meet energy efficient standards.

...this a 10-year ...ajor oil refinery ...Eastport, an ...that would ...erous for ...pertankers. The ...l was dropped ...say, saved.

LEVERAGING ANNIVERSARIES AND MILESTONES

Identify Reunion Occasions

Reunions aren't for schools only. Many types of member organizations could justify hosting reunions.

Examine the various groups that your organization has served, partnered with or interacted with over the years. Which groups have had a common interest at some point in your organization's past?

Select group(s) most likely to participate in a reunion. Pull a handful of persons together from each group to form reunion planning committees. Support each committee's work to plan a reunion for those with common interests.

Anniversary Lends Itself to Celebrating, Wooing Major Donors

When staff and supporters of the University of Southern California Thornton School of Music (Los Angeles, CA) began planning for its 125th anniversary two years ago, they began to think of every conceivable way to capitalize on the anniversary — and the number 125 — to attract gifts.

"Our message was that it may be our 125th anniversary, but that this was about building the next 125 years, and that takes resources," says Robert Cutietta, dean. "We decided early on to get everyone on board with our message being about building our future. We weren't ashamed that our future included a need for money."

"We planned a lot of high-profile events for people who gave, which provided many opportunities to showcase our donors."

They planned concerts with 125 in the opus. They designed gifts with 125 in them, solicited a $1.25 million gift, eight $125,000 gifts, and encouraged alums to increase their $100 gifts to $125 in the spirit of the school's 125th anniversary. Over the course of the 125 days of celebration (Aug. 9-Dec. 11, 2009), the university hosted lectures, concerts or some type of event every day, says Cutietta.

"We planned a lot of high-profile events for people who gave, which provided many opportunities to showcase our donors," he says. "The campaign was very successful and a lot of fun. Everyone got into it."

Thirty-one days into the 125 days of celebration, the school held a celebratory dinner and concert that attracted 700 alumni and donors. "We wanted to hold our first large event fairly early into the celebration to show donors the kind of publicity the campaign would get," says Cutietta. Each gift was announced individually, followed by a two to three minute performance tied to the gift, e.g., if the gift was made to the piano program, a student played a short piano piece.

"Donors loved it," he says. "The event attracted more interest from prospective donors. Alums who hadn't been back for years made gifts of $1,250 instead of the $125 gifts we had asked for because they were inspired by the 125th anniversary."

By Oct. 15, nearly halfway into the 125-day celebration, organizers had raised $2.5 million, all from gifts that had the number 125 in them or were multiples of 125. Two of those gifts were matching gifts that were then used to encourage additional $125 gifts, says Cutietta.

The celebration concluded with an anniversary formal gala dinner. Donors who wished to be acknowledged at the Dec. 11 event had to make their gift by that date.

The cultivation and solicitation of major donors was done almost exclusively in person. No written proposals were used. "My wife and I invited one or two couples to dinner, and small groups of donors were invited to a special dinner before certain events," he says.

Alums received three mailings over nine months. The first alerted them of the 125th anniversary celebrations. The second announced the launch of the celebration and invited them to return to campus for anniversary-related events. Neither of the first two mailings included a solicitation. The third mailing included a specific ask.

No printed material was produced specifically for the campaign. Instead, 125th anniversary logos were added to existing materials. School officials created gifts instead, including crystal glasses and computer jump drives with the 125th anniversary logo.

The 125 days of celebration provided numerous opportunities for media coverage, including a full-page spread in the LA Times, as well as articles in targeted music publications. "We did very focused announcements about different programs at the school that would be attractive to specific publications," Cutietta says. "For example, we talked about jazz gifts to the jazz world and piano gifts to the piano world."

One of the keys to their success was starting really early with the planning and deciding early on what their message would be, says Cutietta: "Our focused, simple message really captivated people. We also got everyone on board internally first and hired an outside firm to help keep us focused. It helped to have an outsider who didn't know anything about the internal politics and limitations involved."

Source: Robert Cutietta, Dean, USC Thornton School of Music, Los Angeles, CA. Phone (213) 740-5389. E-mail: MusicDean@Thornton.usc.edu

LEVERAGING ANNIVERSARIES AND MILESTONES

Diamond Theme Inspires 75th Anniversary Celebrations

It's bigger than a 50th anniversary but not quite a centennial celebration. However, your 75th year of service marks its diamond anniversary. The diamond theme alone makes for a creative springboard for events, graphics and fundraising. Here are a few ideas:

■ **Host a community cupcake extravaganza.** Capitalize on the current cupcake trend with a diamond-shaped display of tasty pastry done in your organization's colors or logo. Invite the public and ask an honored guest to remove the display's first cupcake.

■ **Remember diamonds are a girl's best friend.** Add glitzy fun for a good cause with a Marilyn Monroe look-alike contest, a Diamond Jubilee ala Queen Elizabeth II scaled to your needs, or working with jewelry retailers on a diamond auction and gala dinner.

■ **Look back to the 1930s.** A decade known for economic depression and debutantes, a 1930s theme that also highlights your organization's roots and early

community efforts allows you to choose event themes that range from serious and heartfelt to frivolous fun. You may choose both directions for different activities, to celebrate all that you were and hope to become.

■ **Honor your long-term employees with 75th anniversary gifts.** Consider a diamond watch or ring, diamond-shaped crystal paperweight or framed share of stock in Tiffany & Co. Involve the community by offering similar gifts as contest prizes for those who can submit the best story about your organization, the volunteer who brings in the most new recruits, or the winner of your anniversary 10K run.

■ **Ask young people, "How old is 75?"** Get responses from young patients, students or program participants. The answers will likely make amusing radio or television spots and print ads and may evolve into a memorable campaign to increase awareness of your institution in an entertaining way.

Celebrate Anniversary of Building Dedication

The opening of your new or renovated facility shouldn't close the doors on recognition.

A 20th anniversary celebration of the Fletcher Library on Arizona State University's West Campus (Phoenix, AZ) in March 2008 recognized the contributions of the Robert L. Fletcher family and the university's 20 years of service to the growing region, says Steve Des Georges, director of public relations and marketing.

Opened in 1988, the Fletcher Library is named in honor of the Fletcher family in recognition of their gift of land to the ASU Foundation. Proceeds of the sale established an endowment that provides funding in perpetuity to the library.

"The (anniversary) event brought a lot of attention to the library and how long it has been a part of the greater Phoenix metropolitan area," says Des Georges. "Any time you can bring a group of people together to celebrate an accomplishment or a milestone, you build a greater sense of pride for who you are and what you do. It was also a great way to reconnect with the Fletchers and others prominent in the library's founding."

Leading up to the event, three six-foot banners showcasing various stages of library construction were displayed in the library atrium along with posters of staff memories. Photo displays included pictures of the library and staff, library construction, dedication ceremony and 10th anniversary celebration. Video displays showed College of Teacher Education and Leadership students interviewing the library's Director Marilyn Myers.

On celebration day, staff gathered for a potluck lunch and viewed displays of the library through the years, photos of 10th and 20th anniversary staffs, and shared predictions of what the library would be like in 2018. A short program at 4 p.m. included remarks by ASU Vice President Elizabeth Langland, Director Meyers, Associate Librarian Leslee Shell, family representative Bob Fletcher and Gerald McSheffery, the first vice president and architect of the library, followed by cake and refreshments.

"The event was staged in the late afternoon to allow more people to participate, but it was also an informal event that encouraged attendees to visit with others who have played a role in the growth of Fletcher Library and the West campus," says Des Georges.

Invitees included staff of all ASU libraries; staff, faculty and students of the ASU West campus; and the Dean's Advisory Board. About 100 people attended, including the library's entire staff, deans of the colleges and all the campus library directors.

The eight-member anniversary committee included the library director, associate librarians, library administrators, a library specialist, a library marketing representative and the events manager for the West campus.

Sources: Stephen Des Georges, Director of Public Relations and Marketing, Arizona State University at the West Campus, Phoenix, AZ. Phone (602) 543-5220. E-mail: Stephen.Desgeorges@asu.edu Janice Kasperski, Associate Librarian, Arizona State University, Phoenix, AZ. Phone (602) 543-8518. E-mail: Janice.Kasperski@asu.edu

Attention-Grabbing Events: Nonprofit Events That Draw Interest and Support to Your Cause

AWARDS AND APPRECIATION EVENTS

Events that honor volunteers, staff and supporters generate a treasure trove of goodwill that goes far beyond the attendees actually sitting in the room. Use your recognition and appreciation events not only to thank those who have provided invaluable services, but also to reach out to individuals in the wider community who might emulate their commendable example.

Appreciation-themed Events Build Goodwill, Publicity

Once your event is over, look for ways to thank its key players that will further generate good will and publicity. Offering your special event's volunteers, sponsors or key supporters a thank-you gift — while expecting nothing in return — helps strengthen loyalty and goodwill that will inevitably pay back through word-of-mouth publicity and future attendance. Here are ideas for doing so:

✓ **Give a custom gift basket.** Contact them by phone, postcard or e-mail to give them a choice of items such as gourmet coffee, chocolates, nuts or sugar free candy; sparkling cider or champagne; plus tickets to an upcoming event or free admission to your facilities for themselves and a friend.

✓ **Offer professional lessons.** Buy a group of your most dedicated supporters an hour-long session with their choice of a makeup artist, wardrobe consultant, golf pro, investment consultant or home-staging profes-

sional. Look for experts who appeal to almost everyone in your database.

✓ **Create a spa escape.** Hire professionals with portable massage chairs or tables, manicure stations, facials or foot rubs. Include services that appeal to both genders and all ages. Offer light refreshments like calming teas, savory salads and whole-grain breads. Choose a relaxing venue such as a large atrium with natural light, running water and plants. Send gift certificates to those who can't come.

✓ **Host a brunch and photo event.** Invite clients/donors and their families for Sunday brunch at a hotel or banquet facility, followed by a photo session for the family, individuals or even a baby. Give them one photo as a gift — in a frame with your logo — and the option to purchase more poses from the photographer.

Use Employee Retirement to Highlight Your Organization

When a longtime employee or volunteer retires, go beyond the cake and gold watch to share the milestone with the community. Here are just some ideas:

✓ **Send an interview/press release to media.** Include the person's career path, how he/she participated in milestones like construction of facility landmarks, or pitched in during a blizzard when 200 people were stranded in your gym. A few key memories can lead reporters to other interesting questions for their own interviews.

✓ **Host a community reception with dignitaries.** Include former board members, past presidents, and local officials who may know the honoree. Take plenty of photographs of the retiring employee with VIPs to send to appropriate publications (hometown newspapers, college alumni magazines, trade journals).

✓ **Recognize achievement.** Honor the person's professional achievements with a separate award, such as

Spirit of Excellence that has nothing to do with the approaching retirement. When you announce their departure as news, they may benefit from the increased attention that comes from name recognition — and you do want to honor them professionally while the opportunity exists.

✓ **Celebrate seniors online.** The power of social media was recently shown when one dedicated fan of 88-year-old actress Betty White launched a Facebook fan page to encourage NBC to ask White to host "Saturday Night Live." You can do the same to honor employees who have been with your company for 50 years.

✓ **Host a party to launch their next career.** Your retiring comptroller plans to open a crafts boutique or buy a coffee shop after dedicating 40 years to your organization. Approach this retirement as a kick-off party for his or her next venture for a new media-generating twist.

AWARDS AND APPRECIATION EVENTS

Honor Top Supporters With a Recognition Award

Missouri State University already offered several awards for academic giving, employee support and the like. Why did university officials need another?

To recognize a very important constituency, Brent Dunn, vice president of university advancement, says in explaining MSU's Bronze Bear Award.

"The award recognizes people who have had a major and ongoing impact on the university, whether through service, financial support or both," Dunn says. "It honors a lifetime of service."

Recipients are endorsed by the university's administrative council, faculty senate, staff senate and student government association before being approved by the board of governors. Recipients are presented with a framed resolution and 18-inch, 45-pound. bronze bear statuette at winter commencement proceedings and invited to address the graduating class.

Working to maximize recognition for both the recipients and the university, officials publicize both the Board of Governors' approval in October and the December presentation ceremony.

Dunn says the award not only honors past supporters, it inspires new ones.

"Bronze Bear recipients include past university presidents, former members of the Board of Governors and nationally recognized philanthropists. It's a very prestigious group," he says. "Winning an award is not what moves people to serve, but it does establish a great level of support that others might strive to emulate."

Source: Brent Dunn, Vice President for University Advancement, Missouri State University, Springfield, MO. Phone (417) 836-6666. E-mail: brentdunn@missouristate.edu

University Hosts Leaders in Management Award Dinner

Major annual events can bring awareness and valuable publicity to your mission while connecting you to people capable of providing significant financial support.

Pace University's (New York, NY) 47th Annual Leaders in Management Award Dinner — held April 29 at New York City's Cipriani Wall Street — raised $605,000, says Christine Meola, vice president for philanthropy. Event proceeds, she says, "counted towards Pace's seven-year $100 million Centennial Campaign goal, which we realized two months ahead of schedule."

This year's award recipients were magazine publishing magnate and alumnus David J. Pecker and online advertising innovator Gurbaksh Chahal. Pecker's award was presented by his long-time friend and business associate Donald J. Trump. Bruce Bachenheimer, clinical professor of management, director of entrepreneurship and Wilson Center for Social Entrepreneurship Faculty Fellow, who first made contact with Chahal when he asked him to keynote a university event, presented Chahal's award.

The event attracted 325 people, including Eric Hillman, CEO of Europa Sports Products and an American Media advertiser, who purchased a table and invited celebrities Montel Williams, media celebrity, author, actor, producer, and MS advocate; Elisabeth Hasselbeck, co-host of ABC's "The View" and author of "The G Free Diet"; and Tim Hasselbeck, ESPN NFL analyst and former NFL quarterback to join him.

CNBC Anchor Maria Bartiromo was mistress of ceremonies.

The event, an annual tradition since 1962, celebrates the personal and professional accomplishments of industry and community leaders as well as the university's continued advancement and promising future, says Meola. "It also reunites alums, and showcases our talented musical theater students" who perform at the event.

Tickets for the black-tie event started at $250 (for Young Alumni), and included three other levels — Contributor ($750), Supporter ($1,250) and Sponsor ($2,500), all of which included premium seating and listing in all printed materials.

Sponsor table packages ranged from $10,000 to $50,000. Registration included the option of making a contribution if the person was unable to attend.

The event began with regular and VIP receptions followed by dinner and the awards presentation. Each presenter introduced a video of the honoree's career. For Chahal, they showed an excerpt from his interview with Oprah that included Oprah calling him "one of the youngest and also the wealthiest entrepreneurs on the planet Earth."

To promote the event, Pace distributed a national press release by BusinessWire. Samuella R. Becker, Pace assistant director of public information, says the event "was also featured on online event calendars such as New York Social Diary, Charity Benefits and BizBash Masterplanner, and gossiped about by Rush & Molloy of the NY Daily News. The San Francisco Chronicle also profiled Mr. Chahal in a story that appeared on the front page of one of its sections, entitled 'Internet Star Chahal Getting Honorary Doctorate.'"

Sources: Samuella R. Becker, Assistant Director of Public Information; Christine M. Meola, Vice President for Philanthropy, Pace University, New York, NY. Phone (212) 346-1095 (Becker) or (212) 346-1637 (Meola). E-mail: Sbecker2@pace.edu or cmeola@pace.edu

AWARDS AND APPRECIATION EVENTS

Awards Ceremony Honors Heroes of All Breeds

Staff and supporters at the Oregon Humane Society (Portland, OR) have found a winning pedigree when it comes to donor events. The Humane Society's Diamond Collar Awards night honors community members — human and animal alike — who have made significant contributions to the community.

Rachel Good, Humane Society development associate, shares insight into what made the most recent ceremony such a success:

✓ **Lunch timing.** This year they moved the event from a seated dinner to a luncheon slot, which was more suited to people's schedules than an evening event, says Good. She adds that a lunchtime event is less expensive than an evening event.

✓ **A Hero's Celebration.** The ceremony's overall purpose is to celebrate animals and people in the community, says Good, "which means it's not directly about us as an organization." She says this format helps guests look at the Humane Society's work in a larger context, which inspires the spirit of giving more than a typical fundraiser does.

✓ **The Audience.** The ceremony is a "major event for major donors," Good says. An event planning committee works with donor relations and marketing staff to ensure the event's important and inspirational message gets to people who can make the biggest difference.

✓ **The Fundraising.** Event tickets were $55 a seat, while full tables went for $550. Corporate sponsorships ranged from $2,500 to $10,000. A video appeal presented near the ceremony's end took the audience through the Humane Society's accomplishments of the past year, and ended with a breakdown of its programs, during which table captains handed out donation envelopes and encouraged people at their respective tables to make their gifts.

The 2010 Diamond Collar Awards raised more than $70,000, says Good, who is already planning for greater success next year by encouraging competitive donations from attendees and encouraging this year's attendees to bring guests to the 2011 event.

Source: Rachel Good, Development Associate, Oregon Humane Society, Portland, OR. Phone (503) 416-5027.
E-mail: rachelg@oregonhumane.org.
Website: www.oregonhumane.org

Make 'Philanthropist of the Year' Award a Special Occasion

Being recognized as Philanthropist of the Year — as many local chapters of the Association of Fundraising Professionals (AFP), Arlington, VA, as well as numerous individual nonprofits, do for major donors — is of course a special event for the recipient.

How can you help make the presentation of such an honor even more special?

Here are some real-life suggestions from local AFP chapters nationwide:

"Our chapter has always provided the honoree with a specially made scrapbook with more than 100 letters, notes and photographs inside. Once an honoree is chosen, we get in touch with his or her family, friends, and all the nonprofits he or she is involved with, to ask for letters of congratulations, of memories, etc. The scrapbook often has old photos, newspaper articles, and letters from the mayor and governor. It always includes the invitation and the program from the honoring ceremony. Many times, it has drawings from the honoree's children and grandchildren. Honorees have told us that they keep it out at all times. It becomes a treasured family keepsake."

— *Jenni Venema, Director of Development,*
Illinois Quad Cities Chapter (Moline, IL)

"Every other year, our local chapter hosts a big awards ceremony and luncheon on National Philanthropy Day to recognize Outstanding Philanthropist, Outstanding Volunteer Fundraiser, Outside Youth/Youth Group in Philanthropy, Outside AFP Chapter Member Philanthropist and Outstanding Planned Giving Philanthropist. On the off years, we hold a smaller, more intimate luncheon where we invite the Outstanding Philanthropist recipient from the previous year to come as the guest speaker and share his or her story. Spreading the recognition over two years makes it more meaningful, as the Outstanding Philanthropist has usually been involved in community philanthropy for many years."

— *Martha E. Connor, Vice President of Programming,*
Yosemite Valley Chapter (Modesto, CA)

"Each of our five philanthropy awards is presented to the current honoree by a past honoree. In addition, the past honoree who serves as presenter is asked to elaborate on the current honoree's philanthropy. This has proven meaningful to our honorees — they get to hear how their work inspires others, and feel a part of the philanthropic community."

— *Del Martin, Philanthropist of the Year Award Chairperson,*
Greater Atlanta Chapter (Atlanta, GA)

AWARDS AND APPRECIATION EVENTS

Organization Combines Donor, Volunteer Recognition Events

Staff with the American Red Cross of the Quad Cities Area (Moline, IL) took a chance combining the organization's volunteer and donor recognition events to create a single event that enjoyed overwhelming success.

"Everyone was delighted with the event and all indicated that it was a great way for both volunteers and donors to feel more like one unit," says Patti Franklin, director of public support. "We will continue to do a combined event in the future, and I would encourage other organizations to plan one. Not only is it cost effective, but it gives both donors and volunteers another perspective on the organization they already support, and it deepens the relationship each has with the organizational mission."

The move to combine the two events came at the suggestion of a volunteer as the planned giving committee was trying to set a date for the donor recognition event.

"In the discussion, everyone realized that it would save money and help donors and volunteers understand more deeply how both types of gifts ensure the stability of the organization," Franklin says. "We were able to save substantially by combining the events. Plus, it was a wonderful educational opportunity for both donors and volunteers."

The Red Cross chapter invited members of its Legacy Society (planned gift donors) and Clara Barton Society (those making an annual gift of $1,000 or more), as well as all volunteers. The recognition event, which ran from 5 to 7 p.m., included heavy hors d'oeuvres, coffee, punch and a cash bar.

The program highlighted each of the groups in attendance:

✓ Volunteers with increments of five years of service received service pins. Additionally, a volunteer shared his reasons for volunteering as well as his experiences with the 2008 hurricane relief efforts.

✓ Members of the Clara Barton Society received pins and attendees learned about the society.

✓ Attendees learned the qualifications to be members of the Legacy Society as current members came forward.

Following the event, Franklin says volunteers and staff members contacted 53 of the 140 attendees for feedback.

From the volunteer perspective, she says: "A wider Red Cross audience saw, heard and appreciated what they spend many hours doing each year. One volunteer remarked that he was amazed to see how many volunteers work in the other programs and services at the Red Cross. Another said that he learned how big our Red Cross chapter is and how well it is supported financially."

On the flip side, Franklin says: "Donors had the opportunity to talk informally to volunteers about what they do and heard about their passion for the work they donate to the community through Red Cross. Some donors have inquired about volunteering since the event. One donor indicated that, 'it added a lot for donors to see what is going on at Red Cross.' Two said that the event spoke to how important volunteers are to Red Cross that they continue to give their time for more than 60 years."

Another benefit of the combined event has been an increase in the attendance at Red Cross 101 sessions, one-hour meetings to learn more about the organization.

"We've held these Red Cross 101 programs for two years but struggled to get people to attend," Franklin says. "After the recognition event, 21 of the 53 volunteers and donors we called scheduled a time to attend the program during the next three months" and wanted to know the schedule for the following year.

Although it is still too early to see an increase in donations or in donors, Franklin is optimistic, as feedback has been so positive. She says the chapter is planning an upcoming ask that involves multi-year financial pledges. Many of those asked will be those cultivated through the combined recognition event and the Red Cross 101 sessions.

Source: Patti Franklin, Director of Public Support, American Red Cross of the Quad Cities Area, Moline, IL. Phone (309) 743-2166. E-mail: franklinp@usa.redcross.org

Honor Retiring CEO With Memorable Celebration

A CEO who has been the heart and soul of your organization is retiring after years of service. You want to give him a memorable send-off where all the friends and admirers he has gained through the decades can wish him well. Here are some ideas:

✓ **Commission a portrait and hold an unveiling**. Gather flattering photos of his/her accomplishments to give to an artist who will paint a collage of achievement. Use the best image as the focal point.

✓ **Give buttons, balloons and candy**. Badges, balloons and even personalized candy bars are a few items you can order in bulk for party guests to enjoy.

✓ **Invite the governor or the mayor.** Even if high-level elected officials cannot attend, they may be able to designate a special day in your CEO's honor, deliver a plaque or proclamation. Remember all the valuable contacts your CEO has made through the years. Even the busiest of them will want to be made aware of this important occasion and take action.

✓ **Create a memory book**. Provide themed cards each guest can complete with a favorite short story, congratulations or special wishes. Save the cards in a box cataloged by department, years of service or relationship for your honoree to browse through in the days and years ahead.

AWARDS AND APPRECIATION EVENTS

Recognize Top Mentors

Mentors comprise a large part of the volunteer program at the Community Partnership for Children (Daytona Beach, FL). Each year, the organization — dedicated to child protection through services, mentoring and advocating for children in need — recognizes a local volunteer with the Distinguished Friend of Children award.

"We believe it is important to recognize our mentors because they are such a valuable part of helping to heal a child," says Jo Lynn Deal, chief communications officer. "Mentors are terrific advocates for children and the program and by them sharing their positive experiences, we're able to recruit many new mentors to the program."

The organization currently has 14 mentors matched with children and nine in the screening process awaiting a match.

The award program helps draw welcome attention to the program, she says.

"Recognizing top performers can serve as a wonderful recruitment tool for new mentors and a training opportunity for existing mentors. By nature, our mentors are people who want to help, and this also includes helping each other to be successful mentors."

The organization also recognizes mentors in its newsletter, on its website, through news coverage and media outreach, plus through weekly correspondence and encouraging feedback. Twice each year a mentor dinner is held to bring all mentors together to network and celebrate their accomplishments.

Source: Susan Hiltz, Mentor Service Coordinator; Jo Lynn Deal, Chief Communications Officer, Community Partnership for Children, Daytona Beach, FL. Phone (386) 547-2293. E-mail: Jolynn.Deal@cbcvf.org. Website: www.communitypartnershipforchildren.org

Award Encourages Faculty Fundraising

The University of Arizona Foundation (Tucson, AZ) developed the Eugene G. Sander Endowed Faculty Fundraising Award in 2008 to encourage faculty members to become involved in fundraising.

The award honors Eugene G. Sander, dean of the College of Agriculture and Life Sciences, who founded and for 21 years chaired, the Deans Plus Development Committee, which encouraged active fundraising involvement at college and department levels.

Sander has helped raise tens of millions of dollars in private contributions, says John C. Brown, director of communication and marketing.

The award acknowledges University of Arizona (UA) faculty members who demonstrate extraordinary leadership in fundraising that benefits university programs. Nominations are sought from the entire university community between July 1 and October 1 for faculty who played an instrumental role in development during the previous fiscal year. The selection committee includes the presidents of the University of Arizona Foundation, the provost, and the senior vice president of development and university campaigns.

Award recipients receive a certificate and a one-time payout from a UA Foundation endowment fund to be used for professional development or to support and build the fundraising program for the recipient's college or department. The foundation board of trustees presents the award to the recipient at an annual dinner and reception.

The award's first recipient is Soyeon Shim, director of the School of Family and Consumer Sciences. Shim received the honor in 2008 for spearheading a $25 million fundraising campaign to build the new McClelland Park building to house the John and Doris Norton School of Family and Consumer Sciences.

The 2009 award recipient was John W. Olsen, regent's professor in anthropology and former department chair of the School of Anthropology. Olsen, the JE Tsongkapa Chair in Anthropology, raised more than $18 million in the last five years for the school and increased giving to the College of Social and Behavioral Sciences from $800,000 to $5 million a year. In the 2007-'08 academic year, Olsen secured an $8 million gift for UA — the largest single gift the college has ever received from a private donor.

Olsen was chosen from among 12 nominees.

"The Faculty Fundraising Award reinforces to faculty that part of their job is to fundraise," says Brown. "This emphasis on development starts with the president and provost who place a high value on development work at this institution, as evidenced by their institutional endowment of this annual award."

The UA Foundation Board of Trustees endowed the award.

Brown says hopes are for the award to help grow a more visible culture of philanthropy among faculty on campus: "Some faculty might feel uncomfortable asking for money, but they now see it as finding partners. Donors are inspired and feel rewarded by helping to transform a department's research and teaching."

News about award recipients is publicized in the UA Foundation's magazine; on the University's official news outlet, UANews.org; and in an ad in the student newspaper in the last issue of the semester, which is the university's congratulatory issue.

Source: John C. Brown, Director, Communication & Marketing, The University of Arizona Foundation, Tucson, AZ. Phone (520) 621-5581. E-mail: brown@al.arizona.edu

Attention-Grabbing Events: Nonprofit Events That Draw Interest and Support to Your Cause

PROGRAMS AND EXPERIENCES THAT MAKE AN IMPACT

Want the public to have a better idea what your organization does and why it matters? Create a program that lets them experience it for themselves! Engaging outreach programs are a great way to attract potential supporters, familiarize them with your mission and pave the way for future assistance.

'Day in the District' Shows Local Leaders a Day in the Life

If you're looking for a way to show that donor dollars are being used in a quality and efficient manner, consider offering opportunities for donors to shadow some of your workers.

That's what the staff at the Harris County Hospital District (HCHD) Foundation (Houston, TX) has done with their Day in the District program.

The program has been a great success. Says Katie Mears, special events manager.

"At first it was hard convincing people to spend an entire day with us," Mears says, "but at the end of the day everyone is convinced it was totally worth their time."

So what is involved in promoting and pulling off a day-in-the-life event that draws both praise from participants and positive media coverage? Careful planning and matching participants with their experiences.

Day in the District provides an inside look at the job local nurses and physicians do each day to serve uninsured and underinsured patients. Participants are individually paired with doctors and nurses for four rotations throughout the day, in which they have hands-on experiences in services such as surgery, physical therapy, psychiatry, the emergency center, social work, pathology and other specialty clinics.

The day concludes with a roundtable dinner and discussion with the hospital district CEO, COO and other administrators.

Participants include community leaders, local journalists, donors and prospective donors. Past participants also make recommendations. Invitations from the CEO are sent out a few months in advance.

Mears says the idea was conceived after they realized there was a greater need for community understanding of the public health care system in their county. Day in the District has not only provided that, but has also helped develop relationships with participants that have evolved into roles as board members, volunteers and advocates for HCHD. Not bad for a day's work!

Source: Katie Mears, Special Events Manager, HCHD Foundation, Houston, TX. Phone (713) 556-6409.
E-mail: Mary_Mears@hchd.tmc.edu

Craft Bar Bonds Membership Community

Organize a hands-on event related to your mission to offer an entertaining, engaging way to strengthen your membership community and raise community awareness.

The Museum of Craft and Folk Art (San Francisco, CA) has introduced a Craft Bar as a new monthly offering to entice members to participate in a social hour of crafting.

Beginning in October 2009, the monthly social hour is a collaboration between the museum and Etsy— an online marketplace for handcrafted items headquartered in Washington, D.C. — to offer this unique social crafting event for members of the museum's community. Etsy officials helped to secure donations for the events while the museum was responsible for coordinating the events.

"We had been irregularly hosting craft activities, and I jumped at the chance to do something with more regularity in order to build an audience," says Jennifer McCabe, museum director.

"Obviously 'making' is the core of our mission," the museum director says, "and we are always looking for ways to encourage dialogue about craft and folk art while including people in more interactive ways."

Museum staffers and volunteers are on hand to facilitate the social setting for each crafting event, which recently drew 300 attendees. The monthly craft bar is open to participants ages six and up. The event works in conjunction with the semi-annual Student Night program designed to attract younger members to the museum.

The Thursday night crafting event oftentimes incorporates live music, a number of crafting projects, free entrance to an exhibit and food.

"People love it." says McCabe. "The first three events we had were free to build a following, and we've since introduced an admission fee of $5 to participate."

The museum director offers the following tips for facilitating a hands-on experience at your next member event:

❏ Have a number of experienced teachers lead the activities. Confirm that they've created the activity before with success.

❏ Create a welcoming atmosphere to include elements such as music, tea and cookies to generate a comfortable, social atmosphere that encourages participants to linger.

❏ Staff the event with a multitude of volunteers to assist in facilitating the hands-on activity and encourage member interaction.

Source: Jennifer McCabe, Director, Museum of Craft and Folk Art, San Francisco, CA. Phone (415) 227-4888.
E-mail: jmccabe@mocfa.org. Website: www.mocfa.org

PROGRAMS AND EXPERIENCES THAT MAKE AN IMPACT

Engage Supporters, Community With 'Name Our Mascot' Contest

Does your organization have a mascot or are you thinking of adding one? Host a contest to name the mascot to familiarize your supporters, community and local news media with the project while providing some great naming ideas.

Staff with Butler University (Indianapolis, IN) created a mascot-naming contest after people were confused about what to call the mascot, known simply as the Butler Bulldog, following a costume theft, says Lindsay Martin, manager, sports marketing & promotions.

"When our original costumes were stolen in August '08, there was some confusion among the news media and general public over what to call the bulldog costumes. Many were calling it Blue, which is actually the name of our live English bulldog mascot," says Martin. "That led to calls from fans thinking that the actual dog had been stolen. So we decided that by giving the costume a name of its own, we'd clear up any future confusion."

After two weeks of planning, they had the contest up and running. They publicized it first internally to faculty, staff and students via e-mail, then promoted it at basketball games, on the university website, on the mascot's Facebook page and on the live mascot's blog at www.butlerblue2.blogspot.com. They also publicized the contest to regional media outlets that covered the theft of the original costumes.

Community members submitted nearly 300 unique name suggestions online or in person at home basketball games. A nine-person committee (administrators from student affairs, university relations and athletics) narrowed this list down to a handful of entries. Fans then voted online and at basketball games for their favorite.

Officials announced the winning name, Hink, at a Jan. 22, 2009 men's basketball game, presenting the mascot with a team jersey emblazoned with the name.

The prize package for the four winners, all of whom submitted the name Hink, included four courtside seats to the game and a VIP experience with parking, programs and concessions.

"We wanted a prize that was an experience, as opposed to just something they would put on a shelf," says Martin.

For organizations planning on creating a mascot naming contest, Martin recommends allowing the public to vote online as it will allow supporters far and wide to participate. In addition, she recommends narrowing down submissions to a handful of finalists that the public can choose from instead of letting them choose from a larger pool of random entries.

Source: Lindsay Martin, Manager, Sports Marketing & Promotions, Butler University, Hinkle Fieldhouse, Indianapolis, IN. Phone (317) 940-9468. E-mail: lmartin@butler.edu

Communications staff at Butler University (Indianapolis, IN) published results of a "Name Our Mascot" campaign with this website article:

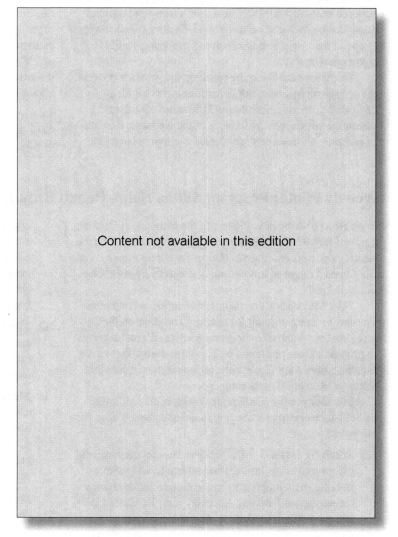

Content not available in this edition

PROGRAMS AND EXPERIENCES THAT MAKE AN IMPACT

Tribute Tree Program Roots College in Its Past

With environmentally conscious moves taking center stage, now is the perfect time to launch a tree-planting campaign to benefit your nonprofit.

Hastings College (Hastings, NE) has a long tradition of tree planting beginning with the first spring planting season in 1883, says Matt Fong, director of alumni development. Through a new Tribute Tree program, Fong says, friends of the college can help that tradition continue.

The program began when fundraising efforts were wrapping up for the college's new science building. Fong says, "We were looking for ways to build the greenscape and let people continue giving." Here's how the program works:

Donors make a $500 donation to the program. In return, the college plants a tree of the donor's choice, selected from a predetermined list, and orders a plaque for the tree, which includes the type of tree and the name of the person being honored or memorialized. The donor's name and a tribute quote can be included on the plaque. Donors are encouraged to attend the tree-planting ceremony and bring family members with them.

To ensure success in the planting and growing process, the college's physical plant department works with a dedicated professor emeritus and the state Arboretum to determine which trees will thrive in the Nebraska climate. In addition, all trees that are planted are somewhat more mature trees, ranging from six to nine feet in height. If, even with all these safeguards, the tree fails to thrive, Fong says the college will replace it if necessary, "though we may make a different suggestion about the type of tree or the location if it doesn't work after a few attempts."

The majority of the funds raised go to the college's arboretum account so the greenspace can be maintained.

While only 10 to 20 trees have been purchased so far, the program is generating much interest, Fong says, especially after the college's recent tree-planting re-enactment. Fong says he expects the program to catch on. "Campuses are beautiful, natural settings. People are interested in things that beautify the campus and live on for a long time."

Source: Matt Fong, Director of Alumni Development, Hastings College, Hastings, NE. Phone (402) 461-7786. E-mail: mfong@hastings.edu

Content not available in this edition

Weekly Winter Program Series Helps Reach Broader Audience

In an effort to draw new visitors to the Museum of Contemporary Art (MCA) of Chicago, IL, and at the same time create an indoor program series during the winter months, staff developed a range of unique and free events from October through April.

"The MCA has a very successful spring and summer Tuesday evening outdoor jazz series (Tuesdays on the Terrace), and we wanted to duplicate a series of similar events to provide indoor programs on Tuesdays during the winter months," says Amy Corle, director of visitor services and manager of internal marketing.

The four programs alternate weeks, each combining performance and art for the programs' attendees. Those programs are:

❑ **Stitch 'n' Bitch** — Held the first Tuesday each month, this event invites knitters and all handcraft creators to bring their supplies to create on-site and exchange techniques and stories. A special guest local artist is on site each month to share work and techniques.

❑ **Bingo/Tango** — Every second Tuesday, this event features several games of bingo followed by a break in which guests watch professional tango dancers and get a chance to learn the steps. Each winning bingo game's configuration mirrors an artwork on view or in the museum's collection. Artists serve as bingo callers and share behind-the-scenes stories participants wouldn't hear at a formal art history lecture.

❑ **The Literary Gangs of Chicago** — This event takes center stage the third Tuesday each month, as local authors and literary performance groups share tales of humor and intrigue.

❑ **Magical Musical Showcase** — Wrapping up each month, this event features some of Chicago's most renowned music clubs and organizations presenting their favorite local singer-songwriters. This hour-long set provides an opportunity for emerging local artists to present their original work.

More than 16,000 guests attend the museum's free Tuesday programs annually.

Source: Amy Corle, Director of Visitor Services and Manager of Internal Marketing, Museum of Contemporary Art, Chicago, IL. Phone (312) 280-2660. E-mail: acorle@mcachicago.org

PROGRAMS AND EXPERIENCES THAT MAKE AN IMPACT

Solar Workshop Shines Spotlight on School

Part of the mission of Midland School (Los Olivos, CA) is to teach the value of a lifetime of learning, self-reliance, simplicity, responsibility to community and the environment and love for the outdoors. One way staff and faculty do so is with their solar workshop.

The solar workshop — a natural subject for media coverage — not only gives students a hands-on experience, it benefits the community, says Karen Readey, director of communications. Plus, Readey adds, the workshop helps expose the community to the school, with more than 200 people attending the workshop since its inception.

Here's how the solar workshop works:

Sophomore students learn about photovoltaic energy during class. Then during the school's Experiential Week, they install solar panels at the school with the help of a solar consultant and teachers. Once that is finished, the school welcomes the local community to the campus, where the students teach them about solar energy and the local environment. Those in attendance also get a tour of the school.

Readey says attendees get in touch with nature just by merely attending, but the greatest benefit is still to the school. "We want our students to be informed global citizens, so the active leadership role completes the learning process cycle in that once you have taught others, then you truly know your subject material."

Source: Karen Readey, Director of Communications, Midland School, Los Olivos, CA. Phone (805) 688-5114. E-mail: kreadey@midland-school.org

Attract Current and Prospective Members With a Trunk Show

Looking for a new event to bring current and prospective members to your door?

Host a trunk show, in which vendors bring their merchandise directly to your invited guests.

Since 2007, The Morikami Museum & Japanese Gardens (Delray Beach, FL) has hosted nearly a dozen trunk shows. The special merchandise sales are free and open to members and non-members alike, with an average of 25 to 50 members attending.

Sallie Chisholm, museum store manager, says she got the idea to regularly host trunk shows after the museum hosted a designer trunk show for an advancement fundraiser: "I thought, 'Let's try organizing some more trunk shows using vendors from whom we normally purchase merchandise and give them a chance to sell more products and share the profits.'"

While vendors are not charged to participate in trunk shows, the museum receives a pre-negotiated percentage of each sale made during the shows, says Chisholm, who adds that they typically purchase some items to complement the museum store's existing inventory.

Jewelry trunk shows are proving the most popular, she says, adding that they are considering combining more than one type of vendor to increase the shows' appeal.
The museum has also hosted trunk shows featuring the craft of Temari balls and vintage silk haori (jackets) and kimonos from Japan.

To publicize the trunk shows, they send out an e-mail blast and hand out fliers in the store a few weeks in advance. In some instances, they provide information regarding the trunk shows to their public relations firm so press releases can be sent.

Chisholm says they plan to create a banner that will

Trunk Show Doubles as Member Recruitment Effort

Since trunk shows offered by The Morikami Museum & Japanese Gardens (Delray Beach, FL) are open to the public as well as members, staff use these events as member recruitment opportunities.

Non-members are encouraged to sign up for membership during the trunk show by being offered a discount on their purchases.

The current discount is 20 percent off their purchase on the day they sign up for membership. Signage is posted in the museum store during the event that says:

"Not a member yet? Ask how to receive 20% off your purchases in the Museum Store for today only!"

---

hang in the museum's main entrance emblazoned with a generic message, such as, "Trunk show this Saturday at Morikami Museum store." The banner will also include the organization's website.

Museum store staff usually helps with trunk show setup and breakdown as needed. Vendors can request 6- or 8-foot tables to display their products, which include fabric table skirts and velvet toppers which were made by staff members. In addition, vendors may use a large mirror and floor easel provided by the museum.

For member organizations considering hosting a trunk show, Chisholm recommends scheduling your shows on days when you are expecting high traffic.

Source: Sallie Chisholm, Museum Store Manager, The Morikami Museum & Japanese Gardens, Delray Beach, FL. Phone (561) 495-0233, ext. 212. E-mail: SChishol@pbcgov.org

PROGRAMS AND EXPERIENCES THAT MAKE AN IMPACT

Program Club Boosts Good Will and Giving

What started as a simple marketing idea has turned into a way to increase revenue and build better relationships with supporters, says Elise Marquam-Jahns, director of planned giving, Twin Cities Public Television, Inc. (St. Paul, MN).

The *tpt*-PBS Program Club is like a book club, with members discussing public television programming rather than the latest bestseller. Members choose from six program clubs — one that meets monthly at the station June through November, and five that meet at Twin Cities-area senior complexes October through June.

People watch a selected show at home and visit a club meeting to discuss it with other participants. Those who attend the station club also hear behind-the-scenes information from a staff person, including producers talking about their latest local or national productions.

Marquam-Jahns says members "enjoy the learning opportunities, the chance to meet others who have similar interests and the chance to make new friends."

The club has also helped the TV station increase revenue. Says Marquam-Jahns, "Many individuals who were $25 to $50 annual supporters have become major donors and/or planned giving donors. Since 2001, 31 Program Club members have become Visionary Society members, including *tpt* in their will or estate plan."

Over the past three years, she says, the giving club has increased fundraising revenue in the following ways:

✓ 86 percent of regular attendees have increased their annual giving.

✓ 68 percent have increased their annual giving by 50 percent or more.

✓ 36 percent have joined the Studio Society, *tpt*'s major donor organization.

✓ 23 percent have included *tpt* in their wills.

✓ 9 percent have made charitable gift annuities.

Interested in starting a similar program? "Give it some time to develop," says Marquam-Jahns. "We started with a core group of eight people. Now we have 50 to 60 who attend the club at the station each month and over 125 attending at the senior centers."

Source: Elise Marquam-Jahns, Director of Planned Giving, Twin Cities Public Television, Inc., St. Paul, MN. Phone (651) 229-1276. E-mail: emjahns@tpt.org. Website: www.tpt.org

Pampering Event Promotes Wellness, Local Business

The Henderson Health Care Services Auxiliary (Henderson, NE) offers an event filled with pampering that not only promotes wellness, but local business as well.

Event organizers invite local business owners to participate in helping the community in a wellness effort. Manicurists, cosmetologists, massage therapists and exercise professionals all join in at the event to pamper the community while supporting the programs at Henderson Health Care Services.

In its second year, Spa Night also brought in an athletic clothing expert and an exercise ball instructor. Tickets were $25 in advance or $30 at the door.

Marcia Regier, junior auxiliary president, offers tips to bring together businesses for a successful community wellness event:

✓ Tap in to local businesses since these are the people who use the health care facility (or other nonprofit organization) supported by the event.

✓ Encourage vendors to bring business cards to give to interested event participants, but ask them not to sell their products at the event so you can create a pampering environment, not a sales environment.

✓ Be mindful of health regulations. Organizers of this event opted not to perform pedicures because of the cleanliness issues and inability to sanitize equipment between clients.

✓ Do lots of advertising, including word-of-mouth from members, says Regier, noting: "One of our members brought her niece's wedding party to Spa Night in celebration of her bachelorette party."

Source: Marcia Regier, Junior Auxiliary President, Henderson Health Care Services, Henderson, NE. Phone (402) 723-4512. E-mail: mmmm@mainstaycomm.net

Attention-Grabbing Events: Nonprofit Events That Draw Interest and Support to Your Cause

UTILIZING CELEBRITIES AND SPEAKERS

Seasoned event planners and consultants agree: Celebrities draw crowds. High-profile individuals — whether at the national, regional or local level — can seem intimidating but many are happy to help a good cause, and there is nothing to be lost by asking. Use the following strategies to add a little star power to your next public event.

To Get Celebrities to Your Event, Challenge Them

Finagling somebody famous to appear at your fundraising event can require endless time, effort and patience — and oftentimes, you still end up with a no.

Turn the tables by issuing a public challenge to the celebrities you want to show up. Then sit back and watch as they work to meet that challenge!

That's what organizers of the Hoops for Hope L.A. accomplished with a one-time celebrity basketball fundraiser held in February at Staples Center (Los Angeles, CA).

Officials with two nonprofit groups collaborated in creating the event: The Arnold C. Yoder Survivors Foundation (Beverly Hills, CA), which offers therapy and support to children and families coping with grief; and Hawks Hoops Sports Foundation (Long Beach, CA), dedicated to providing youth mentoring and basketball programming throughout the area.

With less than a month to organize the event, former NBA player and event co-planner Juaquin Hawkins, president of Hawks Hoops, turned to social media outlets such as Facebook, YouTube and Twitter. Through postings, tweets and videos, Hawkins directly addressed a number of sports and entertainment stars in the LA area, including Magic Johnson, challenging them to appear at Hoops for Hope.

Even a standard press release issued about the challenge encouraged participation with the words: "We are asking everyone who views this news release to send out the official tweet!"

Hollywood set the trend of relying on social media for free publicity, so the result was a turnout of celebrities so large that a line-up of musical acts, including the Billboard-charting Cali Swag District, performed at the event in addition to the scheduled basketball game. An on-site celebrity phone bank was streamed live on the Internet for those who could not attend but wanted to contribute through a telethon.

Hawkins says one major benefit of issuing a celebrity challenge is that the hours you put in double as free publicity for the event and for your organization.

Source: Juaquin Hawkins, President, Hawks Hoops Sports Foundation, Long Beach, CA.
Phone (562) 318-7044. E-mail: hawkhoopscamp@aol.com.
Website: www.hawk-hoops.com

Donors Support Professionals With Endowed Lecture Series

The University of Texas M.D. Anderson Cancer Center (Houston, TX) currently has 20 endowed lecture series.

"An endowed lecture series is a great way for a donor to give money to help a department complement its professional development for faculty and students," says Fernando A. Yarrito, senior director of constituent relations and stewardship.

Donors of endowed lecture series are invited to attend the lectures and luncheons that may follow.

"Participation in the lecture is a good way to keep the donor involved," Yarrito says. Those who cannot attend receive a copy of the flyer distributed at the lectures.

While the minimum amount needed to fund an endowed lecture series is currently $50,000, in the past it was as little as $20,000, says Yarrito, so their current endowed lecture series amounts range from $20,000 to $100,000.

"The more donor funds we have, the higher the amount of interest income generated and available for funding the series," he says. "We encourage donors to give at a higher level so that there is more to spend each year to produce a series. A $20,000 endowed lecture series may not generate enough to produce a series each year."

Lecture series endowments are established as a result of a direct desire of a donor to support a particular faculty member, department or program, says Yarrito.

"While we truly appreciate these endowments, recently we have turned our focus to increasing academic positions (chairs, professorships)," he says.

"M.D. Anderson Cancer Center is a large hospital with thousands of employees," says Yarrito. "It is difficult for the development office to manage a lecture series in another department. As a stewardship objective, however, we make every effort to offer guidance and support to these departments in order for these lectures to be as informative and effective as the donor intended."

Source: Fernando A. Yarrito, Senior Director of Constituent Relations & Stewardship, University of Texas M.D. Anderson Cancer Center, Houston, TX. Phone (713) 563-4061.
E-mail: fayarrito@mdanderson.org

UTILIZING CELEBRITIES AND SPEAKERS

Create a Speakers' Bureau to Promote Membership, Members

To promote members and assist the community, staff with the Eastern Montgomery County Chamber of Commerce (EMCCC), Jenkintown, PA, have created a pool of speakers from their membership of 700.

The EMCCC staff created its speakers' bureau as a place where members can enroll to become expert speakers for events conducted by the chamber and in the community. Members can apply to become speakers and chamber staff recruit speakers from outside of the organization to continue to build the pool of speakers available and to create opportunities to enlist new members.

"We're always thinking about how we can make connections," says Nancy Ischinger, member services director. "Whenever possible, we draw from our membership for speakers and presenters."

The chamber provides speakers for more than 50 events each year, so the speaker database is useful in providing excellent programs and promoting membership.

Source: Nancy Ischinger, Member Services Director, Eastern Montgomery County Chamber of Commerce, Jenkintown, PA. Phone (215) 887-5122. E-mail: Nancy@emccc.org

---

Promote Membership Via Speakers' Bureau

Consider building a speakers' bureau to build and promote your membership. Here's how:

✓ Attend a presentation that features a highly recommended speaker. Recruit this person as a potential speakers' bureau candidate and future member of your organization.

✓ Ask members for seminar referrals. If members have attended seminars that offered excellent presentations by speakers, ask your members to refer those speakers to build your speakers' bureau.

✓ Offer excellent seminars and programs within your organization, and the speakers will follow.

✓ Continue to build a database of speakers so you are always ready to answer requests for speakers.

✓ Promote your speakers' bureau throughout your community to solicit interest and turn those interested presenters into members.

Organization's Theme Ties In to Event — Supporting Literacy

Each year, Literacy Instruction for Texas (LIFT) of Dallas, TX, works to engage and support nearly 8,500 adult learners in their quest for literacy. For 48 years, LIFT has been enhancing lives through literacy by orchestrating 157 classes at 15 sites taught by more than 500 volunteers each week.

To celebrate and support the organization's efforts, the organization hosts an annual Champions of Literacy Luncheon, which draws some 300 people a year.

Tahra Taylor, interim executive director, answers questions about the event:

How are funds raised at the event? How much was raised at the most recent event?

"Prior to the event, we raised funds through table sponsorships and individual ticket sales. At the event, we raised funds by selling individual tickets at the door, raffle tickets for prizes, and autographed copies of the speaker's books. Our last event raised approximately $48,000 after expenses."

In what ways do you honor literacy at the event?

"At the September 2009 event, world-renowned mystery author Deborah Crombie was the keynote speaker, and she generously agreed to allow LIFT to include the naming of a character in her next book as a raffle prize. Other ways that we tie in literacy to the event is to hold the event in

September during National Literacy month and select a theme tied to literacy. Our theme last year was LIFT Off With Books, and the luncheon was held at the Frontiers of Flight Museum in Dallas. We also select one of our adult learners to read his or her story and show a video about LIFT to demonstrate the impact of our programs in the lives of our students and future generations. Last year we used decorated stacks of books as centerpieces and the centerpiece was given to a guest at each table."

At the 2008 event, you were looking for signed books from authors of all genres — how did you use those books?

"In 2008 we received over 300 books. This year we received three book titles without sending a formal request. These books were included in baskets we assembled for raffle items."

What is your best tip for locating authors and getting them to donate signed copies to a fundraising event?

"My best tip is to send the author a request for donated signed copies of his or her book(s). I also suggest asking board members, volunteers and donors if they are aware of authors who might donate one or more of their books for the event."

Source: Tahra Taylor, Interim Executive Director, Literacy Instruction for Texas, Dallas, TX. Phone (214) 824-2000. E-mail: ttaylor@lift-texas.org. Website: www.lift-texas.org

UTILIZING CELEBRITIES AND SPEAKERS

Invite Celebrities to Speak at Your Member Breakfasts

If you have staff or members connected to the rich and famous, look for ways those relationships can benefit your cause.

Staff with the Middlesex Chamber of Commerce (Middletown, CT) capitalize on connections their members and their chamber president — who played with the American Football League's New York Titans in the 1960s — have with well-known individuals in national political and athletic sectors.

Larry McHugh, president and former Titan, says monthly chamber breakfasts feature celebrity speakers who can talk on issues relevant to the county and connect with local business leaders.

Past speakers include National Basketball Association players Ray Allen and Kevin Ollie; University of Connecticut Men's Basketball Coach Jim Calhoun; Major League Baseball's Jeff Bagwell; actor/writer/producer Joe Pantoliano; President Bill Clinton; Rev. Jesse Jackson and U.S. Sen. Christopher Dodd.

McHugh says because the monthly breakfasts usually draw a crowd of 500-plus, they host the events at a hotel with a meeting room capable of holding up to 1,000 people. Cost, including breakfast, is $18 for chamber members and $28 for nonmembers.

"Not only does our member breakfast provide our members with the opportunity to hear a well-known speaker," says McHugh, "it also provides them a great networking opportunity because of the large crowd the breakfast draws."

They promote the member breakfasts through a monthly mailer, promotional flyers sent to the membership and through all media outlets.

Source: Larry McHugh, President, Middlesex Chamber of Commerce, Middletown, CT. Phone (860) 347-6924. E-mail: lmchugh@middlesexchamber.com

Make Celebrity Connections

Larry McHugh, president, Middlesex Chamber of Commerce (Middletown, CT), shares strategies to connect with celebrities for your next member event:

- **Rely on your background.** McHugh stays in touch with colleagues from high school, college and his career as a professional football player.

- **Use affiliations with other associations** (professional, hobbies, etc.) to network and form personal relationships with prospective speakers.

- **Ask members.** You never know what connections they may have that could lead to a great guest.

- **Make yourself available** at other events that feature celebrity speakers, introducing yourself and asking if they would speak at your event.

Range of Topics Highlights Member Breakfast Event

Celebrity speakers for monthly breakfast meetings of the Middlesex Chamber of Commerce (Middletown, CT) are asked to address topics pertinent to the community and of interest to chamber members, says Larry McHugh, chamber president.

Recent presenters and their topics include:

- University of Connecticut Men's Basketball Coach Jim Calhoun, who speaks every October about his team and what it must do that season to succeed, as well as how to succeed in general.

- MLB player Jeff Bagwell and NFL Hall of Fame quarterback Roger Staubach, who spoke about their experiences in professional athletics and how those

experiences related to other life situations. McHugh says the members were able to take those lessons offered by the speakers and apply them in their roles as business leaders in the county.

- NBA player Kevin Ollie, who talked on how he became an NBA player through hard work and mental toughness. Ollie was presented with the chamber's Role Model award, so he also addressed what it meant to him to be a role model and who some of his role models are.

- President Bill Clinton and Reverend Jesse Jackson, who each addressed the members on relevant issues in the nation at the time of their speeches.

UTILIZING CELEBRITIES AND SPEAKERS

Make Your Star-studded Event a Success

Invite a celebrity to play a key role in your event, and watch the positive impact ripple throughout all levels of the festivities.

"We get more generous donations, a boost in offers to volunteer and a more well-received event when a celebrity is involved," says Patrick Sullivan, communications director at the Physicians Committee for Responsible Medicine (PCRM), Washington, D.C., a nonprofit health organization committed to compassion in practice, research and health promotion. Sullivan routinely coordinates celebrity events, most recently PCRM's 25th Anniversary Art of Compassion gala featuring British singer Leona Lewis.

Event planner Andrea Wyn Schall (Beverly Hills, CA) agrees that including an A-list celebrity in your event is a smart move. "They just bring more notoriety and awareness."

The event specialists share points to consider before, during and after celebrity events:

Before: Make Sure Celebrity is Right Fit

Sullivan says to first make sure that the celebrity is a good fit with your organization. "It's not just about image; you need to find a celebrity who not only believes in your cause, but has the time necessary to accommodate your request. There is a misconception that celebrities have it easy; in reality, they have extremely demanding schedules." To find a celebrity, Wyn Schall recommends websites such as www.looktothestars.org.

Once you secure a celebrity, provide that person with as much information as possible about the event and your organization's mission. Don't put him/her in a compromising position where he/she may come off in a bad light. If a reporter asks a question about the event, your celebrity must answer it confidently and correctly.

During: Cater to Celebrity Needs

Celebrities will generally have an entourage of key people.

You need to provide a private space where they and the celebrity can get their hair and make-up done and relax.

Celebrity contracts will often include a rider, or list of amenities the celebrity would like to have provided before or after the performance. Requests can range from the type of furniture to what kinds of snacks or meals to serve.

Incorporate your celebrities into the event, but only to the level that they are comfortable, says Wyn Schall. "Some will want to stay backstage until they give their speech. Others will want to be featured prominently throughout the entire program."

Sullivan adds that no matter how you feature your celebrity, go the extra step to express how their contribution impacts your organization. "Let them meet your key volunteers or VIPs, so they can make that personal connection."

After: Maximize Celebrity Status Through Social Media Venues

The impact of a celebrity appearance isn't limited to event night only. "It's vital to feature stories, videos and photos from the event on your website and social media sites," says Sullivan. "That way you can reach out to the people who didn't attend the event and drum up excitement about your organization as a whole and your next event."

Wyn Schall adds that celebrities generally have terms and conditions on how you can use their image, so get an agreement from them for event publicity and follow-up press.

Sources: Patrick Sullivan, Communications Director, Physicians Committee for Responsible Medicine, Washington, D.C. Phone (202) 686-2210. E-mail:psullivan@pcrm.org. Website:www.pcrm.org Andrea Wyn Schall, Event Planner & Author, A Wynning Event, Beverly Hills, CA. Phone (310) 279-5114. E-mail: Awynningevent@earthlink.com or andrea@budgetbashbook.com

Attention-Grabbing Events: Nonprofit Events That Draw Interest and Support to Your Cause

CONSTRUCTION AND DEDICATION EVENTS

Facility construction is a lengthy process that involves numerous stakeholders and an enormous outlay of financial resources — all of which provide compelling reasons to leverage the considerable public relations potential of a construction project. Whether a ground-breaking, a topping off ceremony, a dedication or anything in between, construction-related events provide a great way to raise your organization's profile and name recognition.

Ground-breaking Ceremonies Highlight Donors, Spark Interest

Ground-breaking ceremonies can spark community and media interest in your construction projects. They also provide an opportunity to highlight your generous donors.

Staff with University of Pennsylvania School of Veterinary Medicine (Philadelphia, PA) host a ground breaking when they begin construction on a new building.

"One important purpose is to publicly recognize donors who make the building possible. It also lets everyone, including faculty, staff and students, know that a major change is coming to the campus," says Gail Luciani, executive director of public relations. "What's more, a ground-breaking ceremony makes a great bookend with the grand opening or dedication ceremony at the conclusion of construction."

When planning a ground-breaking ceremony, Luciani says, having the appropriate equipment and personnel on hand is imperative. This includes shovels to stage a real ground breaking, and key persons designated to officially break ground and pose in photos. They generally ask the building's donors to pose with shovels for photos.

Have a large sign with the name of the building and those involved (architects, etc.) and an illustration of the finished building. These elements recognize those involved and help people visualize the finished facility while providing "a great backdrop for a photo," says Luciani.

Major costs involved in ground-breaking ceremonies consist of shovel rental, tent rental and creation of event-specific signage. Consider purchasing such equipment if you plan to hold ground breakings frequently.

For a personal touch, Luciani says, purchase an inexpensive shovel and spray paint it gold or silver, or use the colors featured in your organization's logo.

Source: Gail Luciani, Executive Director of Public Relations, University of Pennsylvania School of Veterinary Medicine, Philadelphia, PA. Phone (215) 898-1475.

Unique Features Draw Media, Ground-breaking Crowds

Hosting ground-breaking ceremonies for every new construction project, staff with the University of Pennsylvania School of Veterinary Medicine (Philadelphia, PA) know what works to draw valuable attention from both the news media and the community, says Gail Luciani, executive director of public relations.

For a November 2008 ground-breaking for a new critical care center, named after a donor's son who had recently passed away, Luciani says they sent media advisories to local news media beforehand. "We were very pleased with the turnout, which was approximately 70 percent of the 100 invited guests."

Any steps you can take to set your ground-breaking ceremony apart will certainly attract more attention, she adds.

For instance, Luciani says, "In 2004, for the Vernon and Shirley Hill Pavilion ground breaking, we had a search-and-rescue dog dig a plastic dog bone with a message inside it out of a pile of sand and take it to the university's president, who was speaking. The dog was the hit of the day."

Host Grand Openings With Local Flair

A fun, festive, well-organized grand opening will leave a long-lasting positive impression with your guests. Take your grand opening a step further to emphasize the positive aspects of your city or region to celebrate your community and draw more attendees. To do so:

✓ Offer free local samplings. Play up the grandest aspects of your region with locally grown or produced food and drink. Post information sheets that detail the local connection.

✓ Invite a local expert to speak on a topic related to your organization. Check in with the chamber for recommendations.

✓ Create a business-to-business grand opening offering special discounts or trial memberships to other business

professionals in your community to promote your dedication to local membership.

✓ Work with organizations aligned with your goals to showcase all resources and organizations in your region. Consider hosting a co-grand opening.

✓ Set the mood by inviting local musicians to play at the grand opening — a lyricist who can set the mood with up-tempo music or regional talent playing throughout the day.

✓ Invite local notables to speak to the guests — specifically, a hometown hero or native son/daughter who has gone on to fame and fortune but is willing to come back.

CONSTRUCTION AND DEDICATION EVENTS

Share Construction Updates With Donors, Would-be Donors

During the construction of a new student residence and dining commons at Bates College (Lewiston, ME), Doug Hubley of the college's office of communications and media relations wrote regular updates on the progress of the construction.

To share Hubley's observations, staff posted his construction updates on the college's news home page (www. bates.edu/x165427.xml) at least once a month throughout the construction that began in 2006 and ended in 2008, sometimes more frequently if developments warranted, says Bryan McNulty, director of communications and media relations.

A campus construction update also served as an anchored feature in every BatesNews, a monthly e-newsletter sent to about 21,000 alumni, parents and friends, and copied to all faculty and staff.

"These updates became popular with readers," says McNulty. "Doug wrote them in his own voice and developed a following of folks who looked forward both to his information and wry humor in photo captions and salted through the text."

The goals of the campus construction updates, McNulty says, were to:

✓ Generate interest and excitement in the college's major physical improvements (a key message).

✓ Show how the construction relates to a campus facilities master plan. Message: Bates is a strategic and careful steward.

✓ Engage with alumni, potential donors.

✓ Keep the campus community in the know on developments related to the college's major construction projects.

To encourage engagement, Hubley ended each update with the following line, which helped elicit queries and comments: "Can we talk? What do you think about the campus improvements process? What do you know that we don't? We want to hear from you. Please e-mail your questions and comments to: Doug Hubley [link to his e-mail address] with 'Construction Update' in the subject line."

Check out an online archive of Hubley's campus construction updates at: www.bates.edu/campus-improvements.xml

Source: Bryan McNulty, Director, Communications and Media Relations, Bates College, Lewiston, ME. Phone (207) 786-6330. E-mail: bmcnulty@bates.edu

Mark Construction Milestone With Topping-off Ceremony

Is your major construction project stuck between the excitement of a groundbreaking ceremony and the euphoria of a ribbon-cutting ceremony? Why not build up good will and acknowledge key stakeholders with a mid-construction topping-off ceremony?

"A topping-off ceremony is a celebration of the progress made toward completing the construction of a facility," says Gary Friedman, senior associate athletic director at the University of Louisville (Louisville, KY), which recently held a ceremony commemorating progress on a new sports arena.

A topping-off ceremony typically marks the placement of the last or highest beam of a facility's supporting structure. Often painted white and signed by key supporters, the beam is lifted into place amid great fanfare and celebration.

The University of Louisville's star-studded event featured speeches by the chairman of the project's arena authority, university president, athletic director, mayor of Louisville and governor of Kentucky. The 500-plus guests included board members from the arena, university and city, major donors, supporters and purchasers of premium seats.

The event included light hors d'oeuvres, souvenir hardhats and goggles for guests.

While the program itself was not lengthy, Friedman says, it accomplished its goal of recognizing the appropriate people and giving everyone a good feeling about the project.

Source: Gary Friedman, Senior Associate Athletic Director, University of Louisville Athletics Department, Louisville, KY. Phone (502) 852-7244. E-mail: gary.friedman@louisville.edu

CONSTRUCTION AND DEDICATION EVENTS

Host A Dedication Event That Attendees Won't Forget

While major building or renovation projects can be grueling, their completion is certainly something worth celebrating.

By hosting a stand-out dedication event, you not only show off all of your hard work, you make a positive impression that will benefit your organization in countless ways.

So where do you begin planning a memorable dedication event?

First, come up with a wow factor, says Andrea Wyn Schall of A Wynning Event (Beverly Hills, CA), one of Southern California's premiere event planners and author of "Budget Bash - Simply Fabulous Events on a Budget." Whether it is through a unique invitation, a special feature at the event or the entertainment, your event must leave people feeling like they have experienced something special.

In addition to working behind the scenes at the Screen Actors Guild (SAG) awards, Wyn Schall's event-planning business has helped numerous nonprofit agencies through the years. Her best advice for dedication events? Come up with a theme and roll with it for everything from the invitation to the party favors.

One popular theme for evening dedication events, she says, is to "go Hollywood" with lounge-style seating to make people feel like they are in an upscale club.

Another feature that drew oohs and aahs from attendees at a recent event was a large ice luge used to dispense drinks. A fusion of ice sculpture and drink dispenser, the large-scale ice block contains a banked ramp with two channels set in it. A drink, typically alcoholic, is poured from the top of the channel, chilling as it makes its way to a glass at the bottom. To add even more punch, Wyn Schall says they renamed the martinis that came out of the luge after some of the organization's high-profile board members and donors.

For more family-friendly events, Wyn Schall suggests coming up with a feature or entertainment that reflects the mission of the nonprofit. For example, have an artist create a mural that represents the organization in the facility. During the dedication, have the artist on hand to discuss the art piece with attendees as well as media.

You can get more mileage out of the mural concept by creating postcards, posters and stationery featuring the art piece to give as commemorative gifts or offer for purchase.

And when it comes to entertainment, Wyn Schall says that it is not always in your best interest to spend money to bring in a big-name person. Instead, focus on something that is pertinent to your organization. For instance, if your non-profit works with kids, have them come in and perform a dance number or a song at the dedication.

Source: Andrea Wyn Schall, Event Planner, A Wynning Event, Beverly Hills, CA.
Phone (310) 279-5114. E-mail: andrea@budgetbashbook.com

Winning Invitation Tips

One of the most important tasks when planning a major event such as an open house for your new facility is designing invitations that will get the people to the major event.

Andrea Wyn Schall, professional event planner with A Wynning Event (Beverly Hills, CA), shares three tips to make your invitation stand out and create a healthy buzz about your event.

1. **List board members or high-profile people associated with the fundraiser or dedication event on the invitation.** Even if someone is unfamiliar with your organization, they may be personal or business associates with those people and will show up to your event to support them.

2. **Don't ignore the power of e-mail and social media to spread the word about your event.** Create an e-vite and have your board members e-mail them out to everyone in their address books. Or have them post the e-vite on their social media profile. Wyn Schall says that if each of your 10 board members has 100 friends you've potentially opened yourself up to 1,000 more people.

3. **Get creative!** Is there a unique way you can deliver the invites? Some special way you can package them? The invitation is the first impression of the event, and you want it to stand out.

Attention-Grabbing Events: Nonprofit Events That Draw Interest and Support to Your Cause

ENGAGING TOURS AND OPEN HOUSES

If you are looking to broaden community support for your organization, consider throwing open the doors and inviting the public to come take a look around. Well-conceived tours that provide engaging information, access to staff and leadership, and plenty of opportunities for meaningful interaction can be a powerful means of building affinity and ownership.

Keep Your Open House Relevant

The open house can be the most effective and efficient way to raise awareness about your mission. Highly successful open houses have one thing in common — they stay on message. To assure your open house accomplishes what it should:

❑ **Show your good works.** Beyond showing off your facility, an open house is an invaluable opportunity to advertise your organization's accomplishments. Think of your physical space as a map to guide a sight-seeing tour of achievements; set up stations for visitors to learn more about what you do, how you do it, and how successful you have been. Include special guests who can attest to your success, such as experts in your field, or beneficiaries of your organization's work.

❑ **Put a (pleasant) face to the name.** Your organization can be doing all the good work in the world, but without physical symbols to attach it to, that work may not translate. Use your open house to present a symbol to attach value to: this could be a leader or beneficiary in your organization or it a take-away item such as a button or ribbon that helps solidify your organization's symbolism in donors' minds.

❑ **Connect to your donor pool.** The open house is not only a meet-and-greet from the donor's perspective, but also from yours. Include time for your staff to ask donors why they are attending the open house to engage them on a more personal, specific level. Have staff discreetly take notes so you can recall what initially attracted the donor to your organization.

❑ **Get specific about fundraising needs.** Don't be afraid to talk about very specific needs while on the tour; your financial needs will translate all the more when you speak about them in context. You never know when a specific need may fit perfectly with a donor's experience or ability to give.

❑ **Make it your own.** Find spaces, stations, guests and take-aways that are unique to your organization. With the right touch, your open houses can garner a reputation for being a must-attend event within your community. Your open house should be a fundraiser in your mind, but a "fun"raiser in the minds of your guests.

Give Tours That Invite Support

If you do not currently give donors and would-be donors tours of your facilities, consider doing so. Familiarity with your organization leads to involvement; involvement leads to ownership; and ownership results in gifts, large and small.

If you offer tours, analyze whether you are using them to maximize the likelihood of receiving financial support.

To make your tours more profitable:

- Let the public know through all available means that you offer and welcome regular tours of your facilities.

- Train tour guides (staff or volunteers) to recognize giving potential.

- Throughout the tour, have the guides point out projects that could be realized if sufficient funding were in place.

- Make sure named rooms and buildings are properly marked. Have guides point out recognition plaques and mention donors by name.

- Give guests a look at your organization at work. For a college or university, peek into a student-filled classroom. For a youth organization, visit with some young people.

- As you walk between points of interest, interject key messages that point out gift opportunities: "Our endowment is beginning to grow thanks to the generosity of some who have remembered the institution in their estate plans."

- Share messages that demonstrate confidence in your organization's future: "Our plans call for expanding the neonatal department soon based on the growing needs of this region."

- If guests exhibit more interest in a particular area, slow down and allow them to learn more; you may have just discovered their funding interests.

- Take a few minutes at tour's end to sit in an office or conference room and summarize key points or programs and seek guest feedback. Again, you may unearth their areas of interest.

- Send them on their way with appropriate literature and a memento of their visit. Then, send a follow-up note telling them what a pleasure it was to show them your facilities.

Your thoughtful planning and execution of facility tours will serve as a viable strategy for generating additional gift income.

ENGAGING TOURS AND OPEN HOUSES

Educate, Entertain Visitors With VIP Tours

Private tours let you show community members how important they are to your organization while sharing with them both the positive and challenging elements of the work that you do.

The South Side Mission (Peoria, IL) hosts 300 to 400 tours a year.

"The goal of the tours is to give others a sense of who we are, what we do and why we do it," says Meg Newell, associate executive director, development. "All tours are considered VIP," Newell notes. "We genuinely feel that if they are taking time from their busy schedule to come in for a tour, that they are really interested in the ministry of South Side Mission, which in turn makes them very important people."

Members of the mission's leadership team give the tours, which include a tour of the grounds, facilities and ministries at the mission's main campus and a free lunch at their culinary arts training school. Tour guests can also request to visit the mission's off-site locations.

While they currently do not limit number of guests for a VIP tour, Newell says having more than 20 people on one tour can be difficult to manage. In those cases, more than one staff member will serve as host to accommodate the large number of guests.

Past tour guests include media contacts, donors, churches, school groups, college students, prospective volunteers and civic groups.

They publicize the mission tours on their website and by mentioning the tours when any staff member speaks in public. Tour attendees receive the mission's annual report, newsletter and a one-page overview of its ministries at tour's end.

For conducting a successful tour, Newell advises: "Put your best foot forward, but be frank about your challenges as well. No one wants the polished tour where everything is perfect; honestly describe the difficulties that your organization and your constituents face."

Source: Meg Newell, Associate Executive Director, Development, South Side Mission, Peoria, IL. Phone (309) 676-4604. E-mail: MegN@southsidemission.org

Tours Get Major Donors Passionate About Your Cause

In February 2009, development staff with The Clinic (Phoenixville, PA), a medical clinic for the uninsured, began offering donor prospects tours to get them engaged and passionate about supporting the clinic's mission.

The 30-minute clinic tours are conducted near the end of business day, between 3:30 and 4 p.m., and led by Debbie Shupp, development director, or Krys Sipple, the clinic's executive director.

Tours end in Sipple's office, with the opportunity for the participants to chat with a board member and ask any questions.

"Involvement in the tours makes our board members feel good," says Shupp. "I've never had a board member say they won't do it. They are not expected to ask for money, just to tell their story."

About 60 percent of the board has participated in the tours, and the rest haven't only because they haven't had an opportunity yet, she says: "We've only held about two dozen tours so far."

At the end of each tour, participants are given brochures, newsletters and sometimes event invitations, thanked and invited to come back.

Shupp recruits tour participants when out networking at organizations, churches, clubs and the chamber of commerce. "I always give out my card and ask if they are interested in coming in for a tour," she says.

She also recruits tour participants by tracking consistent donors. "I do this by looking at gifts that reflect the donor's care for the clinic," she says. "I call them to thank them for their gift and ask if they've been here. If not, I ask them to come in for a tour."

Once someone is brought in for a tour, he or she is always on board, says Shupp: "We've had donors say 'You painted the walls!?' or 'Wow, I didn't expect you to have done this or that.' When they do, I always ask, 'What were you expecting?' The donor might say, 'Cold, cement walls.' And I will reply, 'We have great volunteers here who have worked to paint all the rooms and keep everything nice.'"

Shupp follows up after the tour with a thank-you e-mail. She also adds the tour participants to the clinic's mailing list.

The tours have been very successful in attracting donors, she says: "Seventy-five percent of those who go on the tours end up making a donation. Donations range from $50 to several thousand dollars."

In addition to attracting donations, the tours have also been helpful in building relationships, says Shupp. For example, she says, one tour participant from a local church asked to be an outreach partner for the clinic, and another asked to help with the clinic's wish list.

Source: Debbie Shupp, Development Director, The Clinic, Phoenixville, PA. Phone (610) 935-1134, ext. 24. E-mail: dshupp@theclinicpa.org

ENGAGING TOURS AND OPEN HOUSES

Engaging Guests Fosters Tour Participation

Offering tours is a sure way to get folks talking about your member-based organization.

Nina Simon, museum designer and founder of Museum 2.0 (Santa Cruz, CA) — a blog dedicated to exploring the advances in cultural institutions — recently took a tour of the Wing Luke Asian Museum (Seattle, WA), and shares how the experience underscored the importance an effective, well-trained tour guide plays in the process:

❑ *Frontloading with participation*. The tour guide made personal connections throughout the tour, asking all tour participants to introduce themselves and often referring to guests by name, which Simon says created a tight-knit, connected experience and kept the group alert.

❑ *Personalizing the tour*. Instead of simply reciting facts, the guide drew people personally into the stories again and again, asking the group to compare their own and their ancestors' experiences to those she described. When talking about the Chinese men who had built the railroads in the Western U.S., the guide asked each man in the group how tall he was. "You're all giants," the guide said. "The men who built the railroad were only 5-foot-1, 5-foot-3, max."

❑ *Sharing a personal relationship*. The guide engaged guests personally by pointing out her name on the donor wall and a replica of her uncle's dry goods store.

❑ *Sharing prior experiences*. Tour guides who recount past tour groups' experiences will also engage the audience. While the tour guide was clearly an expert on Seattle's Chinatown and the institution, Simon said she repeatedly shared information learned from past visitors, which encouraged the current participants to share their knowledge, knowing the guide would value their information.

❑ *Tailoring the tour to the audience*. Simon developed a design technique in which tour guests are asked to design their own tour by featuring a core number of topics from which they can choose to boil down that specific tour. This innovative technique allows tour guests to tailor their tour experience.

Source: Nina Simon, Founder of Museum 2.0, Santa Cruz, CA. Phone (831) 331-5460. E-mail: nina@museumtwo.com. Website: www.museumtwo.tumblr.com

Holiday Open House Combines Member, Volunteer Recognition

Consider merging a tried-and-true holiday event with member and volunteer recognition to get more from your next holiday gathering.

Officials with the Alice Paul Institute (API) of Mount Laurel, NJ, celebrate members, honor volunteers and reach out to the community in one event: the organization's Holiday Open House. Held on a Sunday afternoon in December, the event offers festive mixing and holiday shopping for members and the community while honoring volunteers.

Guests enjoy an open house reception while receiving discounts in the API gift shop. In the event's last hour, volunteers are recognized for their past year's service by having their names read aloud in association with each department for which they serve. Each volunteer receives an API logo pin as well as a rousing round of applause, says Dana Dabek-Milstein, director of leadership programs.

"The end of the year is the perfect time to reflect on all your organization has accomplished during the year, and how those efforts would not have been possible without volunteers," says Dabek-Milstein. "Plus it gives other supporters and the public an idea of volunteer opportunities available at your organization."

To host an event that engages the public while celebrating members and volunteers, she says:

✓ Invite the public, members and volunteers to join together at one event.
✓ In honor of the holiday season, offer all guests gift shop discounts or holiday door prizes that are reflective of your organization and the gift-giving season.
✓ Announce volunteers by name and present them with a small gift of appreciation.
✓ Display membership and volunteer materials near refreshments to encourage community guests to participate within your organization.
✓ Create a festive mood with seasonal accessories and music.

Source: Dana Dabek-Milstein, Director of Leadership Programs, Alice Paul Institute, Mount Laurel, NJ. Phone (856) 231-1885. E-mail: ddmilstein@alicepaul.org. Website: www.alicepaul.org

---

Host Budget-friendly Holiday Open House

To honor members and volunteers, the Alice Paul Institute (Mount Laurel, NJ) offers a Holiday Open House each December. Dana Dabek-Milstein, director of leadership programs, offers three ways to cut costs without sacrificing style at your holiday open house:

1. Ask a local bakery or grocery store to donate baked goods, tea and coffee.

2. Hit January sales for holiday decorations and paper goods for next year.

3. Order a large quantity of pins (or other preferred volunteer gift) to take advantage of bulk discounts.

ENGAGING TOURS AND OPEN HOUSES

Plan a Tour-of-corporate-offices Event

Want to connect with corporate decision makers and raise funds at the same time? Organize a tour of corporate offices in your community.

Base the event on the traditional tour-of-homes event, applying the same planning procedures for a tour of corporate facilities, especially CEO offices, that the average person rarely sees. Here's how:

1. Identify those corporations and CEO offices you prefer to include on your tour. Prioritize your top choices based on drawing card appeal and decision makers with whom you would most like to build a relationship.

2. Contact the identified CEOs (or other top decision makers) to invite their participation, illustrate benefits and lock in the date of your event. Explain that paying guests will make stops at each corporate tour location to spend about 20 minutes touring lobbies, CEO offices and other points of interest.

3. Involve each corporate participant in planning. Involve each corporate contact in identifying anyone they want to include on the list. Discuss where to focus tour time when each bus load of guests arrive. Iron out details such as decorations, tour procedures, giveaways, refreshments (if offered) and more.

This unique event has a two-fold benefit: you are engaging corporate decision makers in the life of your organization and you can generate special event revenue from those who sign up for the tour.

Valentine Membership Party Opens Doors of Opportunity

To grab the attention of new members, the Beaufort Historical Association (Beaufort, NC) holds an annual Valentine Membership Party.

Planners design the event with the specific intention of attracting new visitors to the historic site in an effort to increase membership.

The membership party, set for 2 to 4 p.m. Sunday, Feb. 7, allowed members of the public to visit all 10 historic buildings at the site, spanning the 1700s and 1800s.

All facilities were open to allow guests to experience all that the organization has to offer. Guests meandered about the grounds, explored the apothecary shop and doctor's office, the old jail, Victorian homes and cottages, a 300-year-old county courthouse and the Mattie King Davis Art Gallery.

The event drew 300 to 350 visitors and required the aide of 20 to 30 volunteers, says Brooke Maharg, public relations director. At the event, staff and volunteers were available to answer questions about memberships and any of the buildings on the site as well as to enroll new members. Guests learned about the educational programs, historic preservation of Beaufort and all other aspects of membership through the organization.

The February valentine-themed event is highly anticipated throughout the community.

"This is the perfect opportunity to see the buildings on the site and learn more about their histories all while eating great food and meeting new people," says Maharg. "This party is a great way to showcase what the Beaufort Historical Association is all about at a fun event. It's the one time of the year that we literally throw our doors wide open to welcome anyone who is interested in learning more about the historic site."

Follow these tips for a prospective member party:

✓ Plan the event on or near Valentine's Day (or other holiday) each year so the community comes to expect and anticipate the event.

✓ Plan invitations and decorations incorporating an appropriate party theme.

✓ Host a featured guest who will draw a crowd. The Beaufort Historic Site hosts a featured artist who displays his or her work and meets guests, which Maharg says has become a big draw for the event.

Source: Brooke Maharg, Beaufort Historical Association, Beaufort, NC. Phone (252) 728-5225.
E-mail: beauforthistoricsite@earthlink.net.
Website: www.beauforthistoricsite.org

Attention-Grabbing Events: Nonprofit Events that Draw Interest and Support to Your Cause. Edited by Scott C. Stevenson. © 2011 Stevenson, Inc. Published 2011 by Stevenson, Inc.

Attention-Grabbing Events: Nonprofit Events That Draw Interest and Support to Your Cause

REACHING OUT THROUGH VOLUNTEER-FOCUSED EVENTS

If, as has often been observed, investment begins with involvement, few constituencies are more important than an organization's volunteer base. Development and nurturing of these supporters is unquestionably critical, but events that recruit, educate, and celebrate volunteers can also build a more general awareness of your organization and draw attention to the devotion and loyalty it inspires.

Combine Volunteer Appreciation With Education

The Lakes of Missouri Volunteer Program (LMVP), Columbia, MO, combines volunteer appreciation with education. In April 2009, LMVP staff organized a volunteer appreciation event that included speakers and presentations in an effort to promote volunteer education in addition to acknowledging the efforts of their ever-important volunteers.

Tony Thorpe, LMVP's volunteer coordinator, answers questions about the event:

How many volunteers do you have? How many attended the volunteer appreciation event?

"We have about 100 to 150 volunteers in our group. While we have 80 to 100 active volunteers with training, there are many more people who accompany our volunteers and assist. We're a statewide program, with volunteers spread out all over the state. At our volunteer appreciation event we hosted about 30 people, traveling from up to 250 miles away."

In what ways did you show appreciation to volunteers at the event?

"We give fleece pullovers to volunteers who have been with the program for five years.... Our 10-year volunteers receive binoculars.... We gave a husband-and-wife team who clocked 15 years a handheld GPS unit. We also purchased a few things and got a few others donated to hand out as door prizes. We tried to get a few nice items rather than a bunch of throwaway things. After every couple of presentations we'd break for snacks and coffee, then use the door prizes to get folks back to their seats. It worked very well!"

What educational offerings were held at the event?

"We arranged for presentations, just like a conference. We had presenters from state and federal resource agencies speak on invasive species, fisheries and aquatic plants — a total of three presentations — a college professor talked about the influence of land use on water quality, a 12-year LMVP volunteer who works with a lake board talked about his experiences controlling inputs from the watershed, and the Lake of the Ozarks Watershed Alliance executive director gave a talk. University of Missouri (home of the LMVP) Professor Jack Jones spoke during dessert. LMVP staff gave a few talks throughout the day concerning LMVP data, using the data for developing nutrient criteria and reservoir hydrology. We wrapped up with an interactive session regarding where the volunteers want to take LMVP."

What advice do you have for combining appreciation and education at volunteer events?

1. **"Involve volunteers in the planning of the event.** This was an amazing help! I handpicked a group of volunteers from across the state to assist in event planning. We had a sit-down lunch meeting one day and ironed out what types of presentations they wanted to hear, where we should have the meeting (important for a statewide project), how to best spend our budget, etc. I was amazed at how much more science these folks were hungry for. I had completely underestimated their ability to digest hard science. So, that leads us to the next point:

2. **"Don't underestimate the volunteers when planning the educational component.** As stated above, I wasn't prepared for how eager the volunteers would be to learn the hard stuff. In the planning phase we asked the volunteers what types of talks they wanted to hear and what questions they'd like to have answered by the speakers. They came up with some complex questions! We summarized their questions and gave them to the presenters early on so the presentations could be tailored to the event.

3. **"Start planning sooner rather than later.** Buildings may fill up and caterers might get booked before you can get to them, but even more importantly the volunteers' calendars fill up quickly. Many of our volunteers are retired and I am always surprised at how busy retired people are! They are filling their calendars up several months in advance, and if you're not on there early, you get left behind!

4. **"Give them breaks during the event.** Whether to go to the bathroom or just get the circulation going in their legs, people need a break. And be sure to offer guests drinks and snacks, too. You'll find them gathering near the food talking to one another and making connections."

Source: Tony Thorpe, Coordinator, Lakes of Missouri Volunteer Program, University of Missouri, Columbia, MO. Phone (800) 895-2260. E-mail: tony@lmvp.org. Website: www.lmvp.org

REACHING OUT THROUGH VOLUNTEER-FOCUSED EVENTS

Wednesday Night Work Nights Draw Dedicated Volunteers

Kramden Institute, Inc. (Durham, NC) is a nonprofit that seeks to empower less-advantaged students by giving them home computers. With volunteer help, the institute collects, refurbishes and reuses outdated computers extending their useful lives.

Every week, the nonprofit hosts Wednesday Work Nights dedicated to refurbishing computers for underprivileged K-12 students in the region. Wednesday Work Nights run from 5 to 9 p.m., drawing about 25 to 30 volunteers each week, for a total of about 120 volunteer helpers each month. Summer draws even more help each week with about 50 volunteers lending a hand at each work session.

Due to the nature of the volunteer work, computer-skilled volunteers and non-skilled volunteers are needed at the event.

"Kramden has volunteers of all technical abilities, from geeks to non-geeks," says Alexandra Cordero, director of events. "Non-geeky volunteers can help with equipment cleaning and administrative duties such as data entry. We also invite our non-geeky volunteers to try our refurbishing process. We provide instruction sheets and have a great volunteer technology team that helps all of our volunteers, regardless of tech experience, feel comfortable with what they are doing."

Cordero offers tips for organizing a regular volunteer event such as this:

- Ask your veteran volunteers to tell friends, neighbors and family about their volunteer experience at your nonprofit to solicit more help.

- Make sure your regular event is posted on Internet websites, community flyers and within your organization to draw the eye of new volunteers.

- The more publicity the organization has, the more likely community members will want to be a part of your cause. Encourage news outlets and local broadcast stations to cover your events by sending out press releases frequently.

- Entice volunteers by serving a meal during the event. Offering a simple meal draws more volunteers, particularly younger, tech-savvy volunteers, and gives people the freedom to volunteer without being concerned about fitting in mealtime. Kramden's volunteers receive pizza and beverages, with most of the expenses covered by the organization. Volunteers are encouraged to give a donation to cover the cost of food.

- Hold work night events every week at a set time to draw the most helpful hands. Keep the event atmosphere open-door so volunteers can come and go as needed.

Source: Alexandra Cordero, Director of Events, Kramden Institute, Durham, NC. Phone (919) 293-1133. E-mail: acordero@kramden.org

Appreciation Event Celebrates Volunteer Accomplishments

Each year 2,000 volunteers lend a hand at Meals on Wheels Greenville County (Greenville, SC). The organization says thanks with an annual volunteer appreciation event.

At recent event, titled 2009 Breakfast of Champions — Everyday People, Extraordinary Accomplishments, featured "The Biggest Loser" contestant Amy Parham, who spoke of great things ordinary people can accomplish with determination and hard work.

"There are so many heroes — fireman, soldiers, policemen, doctors and unsung heroes like our volunteers everyday people who do extraordinary things," says Jan Dewar, director of volunteer services, in explaining the event's theme.

Dewar shares her tips for hosting a successful volunteer appreciation event:

✓ Host an appreciation breakfast to allow for the most volunteers to attend.

✓ Draw a well-known, inspirational speaker. Find out

who within your organization knows someone willing to address your volunteers. Think outside the box to determine who within your community could address volunteers in an inspirational way.

✓ Organize a committee led by a passionate employee who will put in the time to create an appreciation event that relays how important volunteers are. Shelley Di-Marco, food service manager, headed up Meals on Wheels' most recent event, overseeing a committee that solicited door prizes.

✓ Provide items for volunteers to take home. Attendees of the Meals on Wheels event received a canvas bag, bottled water, hand sanitizer and a pen.

Source: Jan Dewar, Director of Volunteer Services, Meals on Wheels Greenville County, Greenville, SC. Phone (864) 233- 6565. E-mail: janice@mowgvl.org. Website: www.mealsonwheelsgreenville.org

REACHING OUT THROUGH VOLUNTEER-FOCUSED EVENTS

Volunteer-assisted Story Project Strengthens Organization

Staff and volunteers at Seattle Children's Hospital (Seattle, WA) gathered 700 moving stories from patients through its Children's Story Project.

Through the program that began in 2006, hundreds of people from the hospital's service region have shared personal experiences, memories and reflections about their experiences at the hospital, creating a historical archive that honors more than a century of stories providing hope, care and cures for children and families throughout the Northwest.

Mirtha Vaca-Wilkens, media project manager at the hospital, shares details about the project and how volunteers were instrumental in its process:

How long did the project take to complete?

"The project was initiated as part of the public phase of the Campaign for Children's Hospital and was presented as another way for people to give back to the hospital. It officially launched in February 2006 as part of the public launch of the campaign for Children's and culminated September 2008. The Story Project is still collecting stories to this day ... so the project has completed its initial function as a tool to engage the community in our campaign, but it's taken on a life of its own now. People are still submitting stories every day."

What roles did volunteers play in this project?

"In order to have great, robust content when we launched the site, we had to pre-populate the site with stories we collected. As part of this process, we had to sift through tons of personal thank-you letters written to the hospital, calls that had been recorded and transcribed and had to follow up with actual interviews with people we wanted to include on the website. We worked with two volunteers who helped us track down the best stories and who helped us interview people and transcribe their stories to the website. They also followed up with many of these people and kept them engaged in the campaign. Moreover, we had a phone number for those who weren't comfortable submitting their story

online. A volunteer would listen to these stories over the phone, transcribe them and post them to the website. Finally, we had a variety of events tied to the campaign where we would make a public appearance with our tape recorder in hand. At many of these events, we were able to interview people and share their story on the website."

How did you go about gaining volunteer help for this project?

"We have a great team of volunteers. All I did was ask Denise Green, our volunteer director, to provide a few people she thought would be interested in helping us with this project. In no time, I had the volunteer help I needed."

How many volunteers helped with this project? How many hours did volunteers contribute to the project?

"Two volunteers helped and they worked for about six months during the peak phase of the project (when we were collecting the most stories to pre-populate the website). I'd say they probably averaged about 15 to 20 hours per month during that six-month period."

How has this project strengthened your organization and the vital role that volunteers play at Seattle Children's Hospital?

"The Story Project has engaged our internal community in ways we never imagined. It really has brought home the concept that everyone has a story to share. It has also kept us mission-focused and helped to strengthen the resolve that many of us have in ensuring we provide the best pediatric care for our families. Hearing the amazing challenges many of our families face and also the incredible accomplishments their kiddos are able to make despite their diagnosis is both a humbling and character-building experience. It definitely is a reminder of why we come into work every day. The volunteers embody this way of thinking just by the very nature of their role with the hospital.... This project just helped illustrate their passion for this organization even further."

Source: Mirtha Vaca Wilkens, Media Project Manager, Seattle Children's Hospital, Seattle, WA. Phone (507) 645-8866. E-mail: mirtha.vaca-wilkens@seattlechildrens.org

Luncheon Series Provides Boost for Volunteerism

To encourage event attendance, offer events that do double duty.

Angie Hoschouer, special events and public relations coordinator, YWCA Dayton (Dayton, OH), coordinates professional enrichment luncheon series that expose people to the work of the organization while providing outstanding networking opportunities to local career women and assisting them in personal and professional development.

Tickets for the series are $30 per person, with proceeds going to help the YWCA's mission, programs and services.

Hoschouer notes that the September 2009 luncheon offered insight into how volunteering can boost a resume and make connections that may assist in a job search.

Source: Angie Hoschouer, Special Events and Public Relations Coordinator, YWCA Dayton, Dayton, OH. Phone (937) 461-5550. E-mail: ahoschouer@ywcadayton.org

REACHING OUT THROUGH VOLUNTEER-FOCUSED EVENTS

Hold Raffle to Fund Volunteer Recognition

Look for creative, crowd-pleasing ways to generate attention and funds for your volunteer program.

At the Steppingstone Museum (Havre de Grace, MD), for example, an annual raffle helps raise money for recognition programs for its 100 regular volunteers who serve the 300 members of the museum.

The recognition programs help keep volunteers motivated and serve as a way to thank them for their service, says Linda Noll, executive director. Volunteers are recognized each quarter with gifts of T-shirts, hats or other small tokens based on the number of hours they've served within that time frame. At the museum's annual dinner and volunteer awards ceremony, volunteers receive awards for hours served that year.

"Museum programs such as school tours and other educational programs, not to mention all special events, would not be possible without our volunteers," Noll says.

The museum holds an annual raffle to cover the expense of their volunteer recognition program. Museum artisans donate a handcrafted item for the raffle so there are at least six raffle prizes available. Raffle tickets are sold to the membership and to the public with approximately 800 tickets sold at $1 each, raising a total of $800 each year.

Noll recommends tips to host a successful volunteer recognition raffle:

1. Offer raffle items that are truly unique or handcrafted, making them a one-of-a-kind, desirable item to participants.

> ### More Creative Recognition Ideas
>
> In addition to recognizing volunteers through special events and awards, Linda Noll, executive director at Steppingstone Museum (Havre de Grace, MD), shares other ways she and her colleagues recognize volunteers:
>
> - Giving volunteers a sense of ownership in the museum. If volunteers feel they are an instrumental part of the organization, they will tell their friends and family about the museum and possibly recruit them as volunteers as well.
>
> - Ask volunteers to serve on the board and on committees.
>
> - Enlist volunteer suggestions and assistance to help with special events and tours at your organization.

2. Offer more than one item in the raffle, making the buyer feel they have more opportunity to win.

3. Keep the ticket price no higher than $10 per chance. Keeping the ticket price low allows for easier ticket sales and offers the buyer more opportunities to win.

4. Make the buyer aware that all proceeds fund the volunteer recognition program. This will add value to the raffle's purpose in the mind of the ticket purchaser.

Source: Linda Noll, Executive Director, Steppingstone Museum, Havre de Grace, MD. Phone (410) 939-2299. E-mail: steppingstonemuseum@msn.com

---

Annual Garden Celebration Features Volunteer Display

Look for ways to jazz up traditional volunteer events as a way to thank volunteers for their service and celebrate your organization.

To honor the volunteers who serve at St. Joseph's HEALTH Centre Foundation (Guelph, Ontario, Canada), Volunteer Coordinator Carol McGuigan plans a luncheon.

The outdoor appreciation event relies on good weather and strong attendance of its 50 to 80 volunteers to make for a successful event held in the garden.

The theme "Volunteers ... Caring, Sharing and Growing," is fitting for the garden celebration, McGuigan says.

As a special tribute, McGuigan creates a display that greets volunteers upon their arrival at the event. Located at the entrance of the garden, McGuigan fills the board with photos of volunteers in action throughout the year and adds inspirational quotes that will move the guests.

Follow these guidelines to prepare a display at your next volunteer appreciation event — the volunteers will feel special for the time and effort you put into it:

- Prepare a three-panel, table-top display board approximately 6 x 4 feet, allowing ample room to display your message.

- Use brightly colored graphics, fonts and borders with a garden theme, or a theme that matches your event, to give a cheerful and fun appearance.

- Keep in mind this special group's importance as the display is being prepared, creating a message of appreciation. This luncheon is devoted to your hardworking volunteers for their efforts!

Source: Carol McGuigan, Volunteer Coordinator, St. Joseph's Health Centre Foundation, Guelph, Ontario, Canada. Phone (519) 767-3424. E-mail: cmcguiga@sjhcg.ca. Website: www.sjhcg.org

Attention-Grabbing Events: Nonprofit Events That Draw Interest and Support to Your Cause

NOTABLE FUNDRAISERS AND FRIEND-RASIERS

All nonprofits hold fundraising events. Not all get as much out of them as they could. Unusual, fascinating or shocking fundraisers — an adult spelling bee, a road race in high heels, a skydiving fundraiser — will not only secure needed revenue, they will generate positive buzz about your organization and the breadth of its thinking and vision.

Celebrate the Unusual for Unforgettable Fundraising Festivals

They say when life hands you lemons, make lemonade. Apply that philosophy to fundraising to put a fun, festive spin on an event or situation that people typically dread.

Take, for example, blackfly season, which hits Vermont each spring.

"At times, the air is so full of blackflies that they fly up your nose and into your mouth when you breathe," says Karen Kane, co-president of the Adamant Cooperative (Adamant, VT), the state's oldest nonprofit food co-op.

So a few years ago, the co-op's members collectively brainstormed and decided to make the most of the situation ... by making blackfly pie! Since that year, the Blackfly Festival has reaped financial and marketing rewards for the organization's fundraising and outreach.

The first festival took place seven springs ago, in what Kane says organizers saw as "a day-long festival that would bring joie de vivre to the battle between insect and human."

Now held each May, the festival is the organization's key fundraiser and signature community event. It brings in thousands of dollars in a single day and is also a huge PR boost. "We get in all the local media, plus out-of-town media. This gives us credibility that ads can't buy," Kane says.

The event unites the entire community — and visitors from across the country — to celebrate "the bug we love to hate," she says. Numerous participatory events include a BFF parade — which they call the Macy's Day Parade of the Insect World — featuring eclectic costumes and performances of synchronized bug zappers. A Blackfly Pie contest is judged by chefs from the nearby New England Culinary Festival. A nature walk along Sodom Pond, the source of the bugs, sheds light on these pesky-yet-celebrated creatures.

Since it's a food co-op, it's no surprise that Adamant makes most of the event by selling food, including black bean burgers from the grill. The group's secondary revenue stream comes from its Blackfly store: bug salve, tennis racket-shaped bug zappers, T-shirts, caps and bug bafflers (screened, hooded shirts that keep the flies away from the face).

What makes the event such an effective fundraising and marketing tool, Kane says, is that "the festival has kind of a cult following. Most come for the pure zaniness of it; others come out of curiosity; a few are legitimate bug enthusiasts."

And where the people go, the press follows. "A writer from the Wall Street Journal came to the festival one year," says Kane, "and there was a photographer from Travel + Leisure, plus a great video that ran on a Vermont newspaper's website in 2007 — all of which have helped spread the word."

Karen Kane, Co-President, Adamant Cooperative, Adamant, VT. Phone (802) 223-5760. E-mail: karen@parisbydesign.com. Website: www.blackflyfestival.org

---

Tap These Fun, Fresh Fundraising Ideas

Want to raise money and get some great publicity? Host one of these unusual fundraising events:

1. **Grown-Up Spelling Bee:** Everybody loves a spelling bee, especially if it gives adults a chance to relive their grade school glory days! Raise money with participant entry fees and/or audience tickets. Add in a silent auction, concessions and baked goods on the side. If your first spelling bee goes well, consider monthly playoffs with a year-end championship bee.

2. **Bring Your Dog to Work Day:** How much do you think a dog lover would pay for the privilege of having his/her furry friend at work? If your agency locale is not appropriate, seek out a supportive business to host a premiere event, with hopes it grows in popularity throughout your service area as workers pay a donation to your cause to have Fido come with on a casual Friday. For extra fundraising, ask nearby pet stores for donations, such as gourmet dog biscuits, snazzy collars or other gift items to be sold on-site that day, or see if a dog grooming salon would be willing to donate its services for an afternoon. Another option if all-day dog visits are out of the question: Host a pet parade or a lunch hour get-together at the local dog park.

3. **"No Dirty Dishes For A Week" Raffle:** This fundraising idea is all about the marketing. Rather than having people go to others' houses to wash dishes, it involves securing gift certificates for seven area restaurants — from casual to formal — to create a raffle package good for a full week of dinners. Whether offered community-wide, as part of a larger raffle or in-house at a business supporter of yours, this raffle is sure to draw positive publicity and much bidding action!

NOTABLE FUNDRAISERS AND FRIEND-RASIERS

Chasing Ambulances Helps Victims of Violence

The Ambulance Chase started as a way to turn a negative event into a positive one and ended as a way to raise awareness and funds for the Family Violence Center (Springfield, MO).

The event is coordinated by Phi Alpha Delta Pre-Law Fraternity – Eric Hutson Chapter, Missouri State University (Springfield, MO).

"The concept comes from the way that lawyers are sometimes jokingly called ambulance chasers," says Kelsey Bartlett, a local college student who created the concept and helped bring it to life. "We thought we would redirect the negative connotation into a positive, and create a fun community event for lawyers, students, and the others to attend at the same time."

During the event, budding lawyers "chase" a Cox EMS ambulance one mile to a finish line in front of the Federal Courthouse.

Runners pay $10 to register and receive an event T-shirt that lists all of those who have donated to the Family Violence Center. Runners wear the shirts during the event and secure sponsorships from local law firms. Bartlett says that connection is an added perk for prospective runners. "Reaching out to local law firms is a great way for future lawyers to make connections to secure internships and employment, while helping a great charity."

While the 2010 inaugural event ran into some roadblocks — trying to secure an ambulance to chase, as well as permits and clearances, at the last minute — Bartlett says she is hopeful that the event laid the groundwork for a successful annual event. One that would allow the event's leaders to focus more on fundraising to help shelter staff continue to make the shelter a warm, encouraging place for victims to turn into success stories instead of statistics.

Source: Kelsey Bartlett, Chairperson, Special Events Committee, Phi Alpha Delta Pre-Law Fraternity – Eric Hutson Chapter, Missouri State University, Springfield, MO. Phone (417) 294-7965. E-mail: Kelsey3@live.missouristate.edu

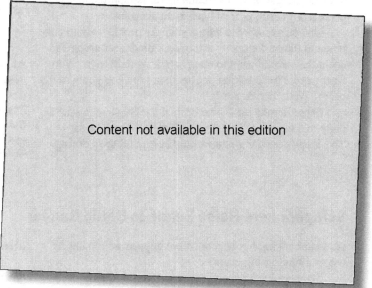

Content not available in this edition

White Coat Day Gets to the Heart of Fundraising

The Holy Cross Hospital Foundation (Taos, NM) has found a unique way to treat heart conditions while also raising funds and building ties.

"Relationships are the heart of fundraising," says Sally Trigg, executive director. To nurture relationships, the foundation presents White Coat Day, an invitation-only, inside look at the people and programs at the heart of the hospital.

Every month, approximately 30 people are invited to participate in White Coat Day. The invitation goes to donors, governmental leaders, media people, business owners and interested community members.

Attendees have lunch, hear some stories from doctors and tour an area of the hospital. Trigg says the attendees receive special treatment while on the tour, wearing white coats emblazoned with VIP buttons. In recent months, the tour has focused on new digital radiology equipment.

Participants also learn about new hospital programs, plans for the future and important current health care concerns.

Trigg says the benefits of the program are innumerable. "It helps the participants learn about the hospital in a relaxed, enjoyable atmosphere, instead of when they are sick or anxious as a patient or a visitor. They also meet hospital staff and doctors and learn more about them and the other participants. It helps the foundation because more people learn about the hospital and about the focuses of our fundraising. It helps the community by increasing knowledge — attendees pass on the word about programs and services that are available — and it creates bridges," she says.

Source: Sally Trigg, Executive Director, Holy Cross Hospital Foundation, Taos, NM. Phone (575) 751-5811. E-mail: strigg@taoshospital.org. Website: www.taoshospital.org

NOTABLE FUNDRAISERS AND FRIEND-RASIERS

Involve Younger Constituents At a Summer Beach Party

Summer is vacation time for many potential donors, making it the perfect time for your organization to host a summer-fun fundraiser that celebrates your organization while attracting new donors.

Brian Kish, assistant vice president for advancement at Salve Regina University (Newport, RI) and annual giving consultant with Campbell & Company (Chicago, IL), says one of the most important ways to promote annual giving is to attract younger donors.

"The earlier you can start engaging potential donors, the better," Kish says. The likelihood of a donor returning to donate to the same institution increases approximately 20 percent with each year of his/her engagement.

One proven way to attract younger people — both current and future donors — is to plan a fundraiser around an event they would want to attend anyway, Kish says. "You want people to be asking one another, 'Are you going to this event? Well, then so am I.'"

Salve Regina hosts The Bash at the Beach — a seaside party in a historical and "touristy" part of town, he says. "We knew younger alumni would be around town during the summer, but wouldn't be coming to campus. So we decided to take the fundraising party to them."

For a summer bash, Kish recommends:

✓ Holding the event at a well-loved restaurant or bar with outdoor seating, a large deck or a waterfront view.

✓ Charging a ticket price that serves as the donor's contribution to the fundraiser. The ticket will earn the donor two drinks, food, parking and a gift. Build the fair market value of those items into the ticket price, with enough left over to earn a healthy percentage for your organization.

✓ Aiming your marketing techniques at younger donors — advertise in recent alumni publications, organizations for young professionals, and online.

Source: Brian Kish, Assistant Vice President for Advancement, Salve Regina University, Newport, RI, and Annual Giving Consultant, Campbell & Company, Chicago, IL. Phone (401) 847-6650. E-mail: annualGiving@campbellcompany.com and brian.kish@salve.edu. Websites: www.salve.edu and www.campbellcompany.com/people/b_kish.html

Scrapbookers Raise Funds to Battle Cancer

As scrapbooking has become more popular, so too has its use as a fundraising event.

Scrapbook stores, civic groups and community members across the nation host "cropping" events that can last a few hours, a full weekend or longer to raise money for the Susan G. Komen for the Cure Foundation.

One such event, The Siouxland Crop for the Cure® (Sioux City, IA), has raised more than $21,000 for its local affiliate since 2007. The 12-hour event features scrapbooking, card making, quilting, shopping with on-site vendors, more than 100 auction items, massages, a garage sale of scrapbooking materials, door prizes and snacks.

Jamee Carlson, founder and co-chair, along with a fellow committee member, got the idea to host a scrapbooking event after attending a similar event in a nearby city.

Inspired by her mother-in-law, who is a two-time breast cancer survivor, Carlson got to work immediately recruiting friends to bring her vision to reality.

With no money for publicity, Carlson says she relied on word of mouth, hanging flyers at local businesses and running a newspaper ad in a local paper to reach her audience. A lack of publicity dollars didn't deter attendees, says Carlson, as more than 60 scrappers supported the inaugural event, raising more than $9,500. In 2008, the event drew more than 70 guests and generated more than $11,700.

To make sure 100 percent of the fundraiser's net profits are donated to the local Susan G. Komen affiliate, Carlson says the five-person committee solicits donations and support from local residents and businesses and at times reach into their own pockets to purchase items needed for the event.

Source: Jamee Carlson, Founder and Co-chair, The Siouxland Crop for the Cure®, Hinton, IA. Phone (712) 947-4770. E-mail: sxlandcropforthecure@yahoo.com

NOTABLE FUNDRAISERS AND FRIEND-RASIERS

Adult Spelling Bee Generates Media Exposure

How do you spell special events success?

For The Marathon County Literacy Council, Inc. (Wausau, WI), you leave the spelling up to the participants in your popular annual adult spelling bee.

The spelling bee raises funds while boosting awareness of the organization's mission to provide anyone with literacy needs the tools they require to improve their conversation skills or other literacy needs.

For three hours, teams of three adults compete to spell collegiate-level terminology. After each team takes time to discuss the spelling of the word, one team member recites the word and the team's agreed-upon spelling of that word. Teams can purchase a second chance for $20. The bee continues until one team remains.

Audience members get involved through a 10-word spelling contest.

Bernie Corsten, program coordinator, says the event is promoted for one month leading up to the spelling bee by local radio, newspaper and TV stations, as well as their website. A radio announcer from Wisconsin Public Radio serves as emcee.

The 2008 spelling bee raised $3,000 through donations made by participating teams.

Source: Bernie Corsten, Program Coordinator, The Marathon County Literacy Council, Inc., Wausau, WI. Phone (715) 261-7292. E-mail: mcliteracy@mail.co.marathon.wi.us

Book-themed Fundraiser Writes a Success Story for Library

An annual themed gala is helping generate major funds while engaging current and potential donors to the St. Louis Public Library Foundation (St. Louis, MO). The gala is part of the fundraising efforts for the foundation's $20 million capital campaign.

Liz Reeves, director of development and communication for the foundation, explains that in order to engage the entire community, the annual events alternate between formal and casual ticketed events.

In November 2009, they offered a casual party that became a colorful and creative extravaganza called Stranger than Fiction: A Novel Affair. "We wanted the party to have a literary theme," says Reeves, "in order to remind people what we are working toward."

The event was an instant classic, attracting 600 guests at $75 per ticket and netting $100,000, says Reeves. She says that sticking to the event's theme proved invaluable in its success.

Specifically, she says, organizers and participants played up the literary theme by:

✓ **Dressing the part.** Guests and staff were encouraged to come dressed as their favorite literary characters. "People really went all out," says Reeves. "The costume-party feel added a lot to the atmosphere of the evening."

✓ **Spotlighting literary themes.** Five of the library's outer rooms were decorated for five genres of literature: mystery, romance, sci-fi, banned books and children's literature. The themes continued...

• **In the food** — Caterers from five restaurants were invited to present culinary takes on some classic novels: Seafood for sci-fi author's Jules Verne's 40,000 Leagues Under the Sea; Huckleberry Finn Tarts and Lady Godiva Chocolate cupcakes for banned book desserts.

• **In the drink** — A local hotel donated creative drink recipes for the cash bar: "Scarlet Letter Lemonade" and "A Oliver's Martini, with a Twist".

• **In the entertainment** — Thematically appropriate performers were hired for each room: a marionette puppeteer in the children's literature room, an escape artist in the mystery room.

✓ **Featuring a musical interlude.** A full-sized gospel choir filled the historic, high-ceilinged marble room with music. "We wanted to remind people that we have a large collection of sheet music, scores and CDs for checkout," says Reeves.

✓ **Offering a Bookworm's Raffle.** Young volunteers went around selling raffle tickets for a unique literary privilege: to have your name used in a new book by one of several well-known authors.

✓ **Sponsoring a Shh-Silent Auction.** Including signed books, author appearances at your book club and one of 14 sets of customized Build-a-Bear Workshop plush critters, dressed to look like literary characters.

Source: Liz Reeves, Director of Development and Communication, and Mike Ryan, Development Associate, St. Louis Public Library Foundation, St. Louis, MO. Phone (314) 539-0359. E-mail: ereeves@slplfoundation.org or mryan@slplfoundation.org. Website: www.slplfoundation.org

NOTABLE FUNDRAISERS AND FRIEND-RASIERS

Scrabble® Challenge Tests Skill, Raises Big Bucks

Frontier College (Toronto, Ontario, Canada) hosts an annual Scrabble® Corporate Challenge to raise funds to improve literacy rates across Canada. The event raises attention for the college and the cause, as well as major funds, bringing in nearly $1 million over five years.

"With more than 40 percent of Canadians struggling to read and write, our Scrabble® Corporate Challenge is the perfect antidote," says Sherry Campbell, college president. "Having Bay Street executives roll up their sleeves to play Scrabble®, shows corporate Canada's desire to be a part of the literacy solution."

The 2009 corporate challenge, presented by TMX Group, consisted of 40 teams of four players playing a rousing match of the popular word-crafting game.

The competition "creates a networking opportunity for like-minded wordsmiths from companies representing banking, legal, accounting, data services, technology and wealth management sectors to gather in support of Frontier College's literacy programs," says Meredith Roberts, Frontier's manager of special events and media relations.

Teams of four players paid $5,000 to compete. Teams may invite up to four guests to cheer on the players. Local corporations funded employee teams, and some companies donated entry fees for other groups to participate, such as a team from the public library.

The night followed a hockey theme, including referees who monitor the event.

At the 2009 event, six regionally and nationally recognized Scrabble® champions were on hand to act as ringers for teams to enlist for assistance — considered a power play — when choosing a word from their existing tiles for an additional donation.

Teams competed for title of best individual player, winner of their conference (e.g., legal conference, accounting conference) and highest-scoring team. The team deemed the final winner overall took home the Scrabble® TMX Cup and bragging rights.

In addition to the corporate challenge, event organizers encourage a grassroots Scrabble® effort for individuals to participate in known as the Scrabble® Friends & Family Challenge. In this effort, individuals can coordinate a neighborhood Scrabble® challenge raising funds for local literacy programs.

Source: Meredith Roberts, Manager-Special Events & Media Relations, Frontier College Foundation, Toronto, Ontario, Canada. Phone (416) 923-3591. E-mail: mroberts@frontiercollege.ca

Puzzle-filled Event Builds Excitement, Raises Funds

Puzzling over what kind of event might raise both friends and funds for your organization? Check out Silicon Valley Puzzle Day. Now in its fifth year, the annual event raises funds for the Morgan Hill Library Foundation (Morgan Hill, CA).

As for what types of games to share, Emily Shem-Tov, foundation president, says crossword puzzles seemed to be a good match for the library supporters. "We also decided to add Sudoku into the mix because of our location and the number of math and computer science folks around that we thought would be interested," she says. Adding the popular number-based game led to a sponsorship/partnership with the American Institute of Mathematics (Palo Alto, CA).

Puzzle Day is actually two days of puzzle fun. Saturday is filled with workshops with prominent area puzzle experts, including sessions just for children. By including these experts, Shem-Tov says, "We've been able to attract some really wonderful presenters, including some of the top puzzle constructors and solvers in the country. Last year the Saturday and Sunday New York Times puzzles the weekend of the event were written by two of our speakers! It was amazing timing and a testament to the quality of our speakers."

Sunday is competition day, with tournaments for crosswords and Sudoku plus bonus rounds of cryptic crosswords and killer Sudoku. Tournaments for both adults and children draw entire families ready to compete with their peers.

Shem-Tov says that while the event itself doesn't bring in much money, "It definitely raises our profile in town, lets us get the word out about our organization and brings lots of new people into the library. Doing crosswords is usually a solitary activity done at one's kitchen table, so people really appreciate the opportunity to get to meet other people who share their passion."

Source: Emily Shem-Tov, President, Morgan Hill Library Foundation, Morgan Hill, CA. Phone (408) 778-1743. E-mail: Emily@chocolatespoon.com

Promoting Your Niche Event

Planning a niche event similar to the Silicon Valley Puzzle Day presented by the Morgan Hill Library Foundation (Morgan Hill, CA). Tap into persons enthusiastic about the niche area, says Emily Shem-Tov, foundation president.

"If you can tap into an existing passion and enthusiasm for your particular activity, those people can really help spread the word," she says.

Shem-Tov says that for the foundation's crossword puzzle/Sudoku event, they post to online sites where crossword people go to play or to talk about writing or solving puzzles, and buy ads on Google and Facebook targeting people looking for puzzles.

NOTABLE FUNDRAISERS AND FRIEND-RASIERS

Casting for a Cure Offers New Twists for Fishing Tourneys

The loss of loved ones to cancer brought a group of Minnesota residents together to create a new Minnesota-worthy event called Casting for a Cure (Sartell, MN).

Launched in September 2009, the event incorporates the joy of fishing and celebration of life for persons who experience cancer within their families. The event is founded by the children of Sandy Karasch, who died in 2008 from cancer. Joe Schulte, co-chair and Karasch's son-in-law, share elements that contributed to the first-time event's success:

Specialty items. A commemorative fishing bobber with the event logo was made available on the event website, with 240 selling for $5 each.

PayPal donation options. Using the online money handling system, www.paypal.com, allowed website visitors to contribute. PayPal gifts ranged from $25 to $300.

Digital fishing competition. Participants paid a $30 fee, fished on any lake they wished, then photographed their catch using an official measuring tool and entered the photo.

Maximized exposure on social networking sites. Organizers spread the word about the event and donation options via Facebook and various other social networking sites.

Special sponsor treatment. Sponsors donating $1,000 received a specialty gift basket.

Awards ceremony and silent auction. The awards celebration included a silent auction of fishing-related items which accounted for a large portion of the event's funds.

Funds raised in the first-ever event allowed organizers to donate $15,000 to the Coborn Cancer Center (St. Cloud, MN) and create a perpetual fund for ongoing events. Plans for future events call for upgrading pro-fishing level giveaways for the tournament and fostering stronger relationships with sponsors.

Source: Joe Schulte, Co-Chair, Casting for a Cure-Greater Minnesota Fight for a Cure, Sartell, MN. Phone (320) 250-1010. E-mail: info@castingforacure.org. Website: www.castingforacure.org

Motorcycle Riders Cruise to Victory in Fundraising Efforts

You might not think that motorcycle riders and sick children go together, but George S. Wilson, one of the organizers of the "Cruise" Motorcycle Benefit Ride for the Ronald McDonald House (Rochester, MN) says you couldn't be more wrong.

"The riders might look rough in some cases, but they have hearts of gold and would do anything for the kids that are going through treatments and staying at the Ronald McDonald House," Wilson says.

That might explain why the biker-driven event has raised more than $500,000 in the last eight years and grown to become the largest motorcycle benefit ride in southern Minnesota.

Here's how the cruise works: A committee of 12 to 15 volunteers begins work 10 months before the annual event to plan the route, solicit donations and make arrangements. Those arrangements include selecting stops along the 132-mile ride, arranging food at those stops, coordinating a live and silent auction and planning a parade that goes from the ride's end point, Rochester Community College, to the Ronald McDonald House.

The committee also secures the necessary permits for the parade and business sponsors at two different levels: $1,000 and $2,500.

Event day starts very early with 30 to 40 volunteers handling registration, staging the auctions, placing sponsor banners and checking microphones and other equipment to make sure everything is ready for the big day.

Wilson says that the committee changes the route every year to keep interest up among the riders, but that it's really the parade and the chance to meet with the children at the house that keep them coming back.

Following the parade, organizers present an oversized check to children at the Ronald McDonald House.

The 2008 event included 1,237 riders — many of whom participate each year — and raised $104,000, helping offset 10 pecent of the house's operating budget.

Source: George S. Wilson, Rochester, MN. Phone (507) 288-3834. E-mail: gewilson@heartman-insurance.com

At a Glance —	
Event Type:	Motorcycle benefit ride and parade
Gross:	$110,000-plus
Costs:	$8,000-9,000
Net Income:	$100,000-plus
Volunteers:	12 on committee; 30-40 more on event day
Planning:	10 months
Attendees:	1,200-plus
Revenue Sources:	Rider registration, sponsorships and T-shirt sales
Use of funds:	Operating budget for Ronald McDonald House of Rochester, MN
Unique Feature:	Largest motorcycle benefit ride in southern Minnesota

NOTABLE FUNDRAISERS AND FRIEND-RASIERS

Branding, Varied Activities Ensure a Dazzling Event

The annual fundraiser of the Los Gatos Education Foundation (Los Gatos, CA) needed tweaking. While the event was raising money, the confusion attendees seemed to have about proper attire suggested problems with branding and messaging, says Kimberley Ellery, director of special events.

The solution? Denim and Diamonds.

"The theme really established the tone of the evening," Ellery says. "The décor was casual but elegant — red roses and crystal — and the guests looked fabulous. They were very comfortable in their jeans, but outstanding in their jewelry."

Organizers wove the diamond motif throughout the event, from promotional artwork to a jeweler selling diamonds (and donating a portion of the proceeds to the foundation) at the event.

While the theme got people in the door, Ellery credits the variety of activities for securing their support. "We were very deliberate about offering many levels of participation at different price points," says Ellery. "People could jump in for as little as $20, or offer thousands through family sponsorships."

The event's many activities included:

- **Chicken Bingo.** A fenced, 7X7-foot grid of 100 squares was brought to the dance floor and attendees bought individual squares for $20. A diamond-wearing chicken was then placed on the grid, and the owner of the square

where it did its business won diamond earrings. Of the event Ellery says, "You could have heard a pin drop in that room, everyone was so fascinated. It was a perfect way to focus attention for the auction."

- **Heads or Tails Raffle.** For $30, participants called successive coin flips until only one remained, winning an iPad tablet computer.

- **Premium Wine Bar.** Guests paid $25 per glass to sample fine wine donated by local vineyards. Five-glass punch cards were available for $100.

- **"Best of" Raffle.** 100 tickets were sold at $100 each, with the winner receiving his or her choice of any single item offered in the live auction.

- **Wine Toss.** For $15 a toss, attendees attempted to ring the necks of donated bottles of wine. Those who succeeded won the wine and an auction item valued at $50 or less. Ellery says, "It's a great way to get rid of leftover bits that can't be easily packaged or auctioned off, packs of five car wash certificates and things like that."

Other activities including a ticketed Texas Hold 'Em tournament, black jack tables, and live and silent auctions helped the event net $90,000.

Source: Kimberley Ellery, Director of Special Events, Los Gatos Education Foundation, Los Gatos, CA.
Phone (408) 402-5014. E-mail: KimberleyEllery@comcast.net

Groups Carve Creative Path in Race to Raise Funds, Awareness

In June 2010, a pair of high heels was the accessory du jour for those interested in participating in the mission to raise awareness of domestic violence.

The inaugural Heel the Sole Race for Domestic Violence Awareness was the result of a partnership between the Theta Zeta Omega chapter of Alpha Kappa Alpha sorority (Ocean Springs, MS), the Mississippi Gulf Coast Black Nurses Association (Gulfport, MS), the Gulf Coast Women's Center for Non-Violence (Biloxi, MS) and the Salvation Army Domestic Violence Unit (Pascagoula, MS).

The race required participants to run a 1.5K race along the Gulf Coast Community College (Perkinston, MS) walking track in high heels. The net contributions of the event went to the Salvation Army Domestic Violence Unit (Pascagoula, MS).

Angela M. McCon, an organizer for the event, credits

its success to many unique attributes, which include its venue and theme.

"The event also worked because there was great organization among committee members and event chairs and great support from volunteers, the community and sponsors," says McCon.

McCon says they plan to hold the event during a cooler month, such as September, or the beginning of November. The team decided against holding the event in October, even though it is Domestic Violence Awareness Month, so that it does not compete with Breast Cancer Awareness Month events.

Source: Angela M. McCon, Theta Zeta Omega Health Committee Chairman, Theta Zeta Omega Chapter of Alpha Kappa Alpha Sorority, Inc. Ocean Springs, MS. Phone (228) 235-7906. Website: www.thetazetaomega.com

NOTABLE FUNDRAISERS AND FRIEND-RASIERS

Signed, Sealed & Delivered — Original Art by Mystery Artisans

To celebrate existing members while getting potential members through your door, consider hosting an event that showcases your mission.

Here's a technique that does just that through an eye-catching, albeit small, size: 4 by 6 inches.

Members of the Silvermine Guild Arts Center (New Canaan, CT) banded together to promote art and fellowship among members and the community with its Signed, Sealed & Delivered event in October 2009. The event raised $17,000 while generating community-wide enthusiasm and interest. Signed, Sealed & Delivered features original works of art by Silvermine Guild artisans, School of Art faculty and invited artists and friends of the guild. Artwork — all in 4x6-inch size – features paintings, prints, photographs, mixed media and collages. Artists sign the originals on the back adding an air of mystery to the event as guests are unaware who the artist is until after purchase

> *"Members are very involved ... from volunteering to help coordinate and install the artwork, to helping at both the Collector's Preview Party and the Open to the Public Sale and most of all, donating their fabulous artwork to the event."*

This established fundraising event has taken place over the last eight years with a public sale on an autumn Sunday afternoon. Three years ago, Silvermine added a Collector's Preview party the night before the public sale, which consistently draws about 200 guests.

Silvermine Guild Arts Center staff answers questions about the event:

Who is invited to Signed, Sealed & Delivered?

An average of about 150 to 200 guests attend the Collector's Preview that is held on a Saturday night, and on Sunday we have it open to the public. For the Collector's party, we invite guests who have attended in the past, donors and supporters of Silvermine, students of the School of Art, other Guild Members, etc.

Who creates the original, 4x6-inch artwork?

The Guild Artists members, faculty, students and other invited artists create their own artwork that can include techniques such as: paintings, prints, photographs, collages and mixed media.

How many pieces were up for sale at the last event?

We had more than 500 original works of art.

Why did you decide to have the artists sign their works of art on the back?

This provides mystery and fun to the event. People like to see if they can find works by artists they are familiar with, or just buy that which they like.

Were artists given a particular theme for the artwork?

No, they could create whatever they liked on any subject; the only restrictions they had was the size of 4x6.

What role do guild members take at this event? What tips can you share about involving members at events?

The Guild Artist members are very involved with Signed, Sealed & Delivered from volunteering to help coordinate and install the artwork, to helping at both the Collector's Preview Party and the Open to the Public Sale and most of all, donating their fabulous artwork to the event. Signed, Sealed & Delivered is one of two major fundraising events we hold at Silvermine, and is of great value and importance to the arts center in supporting the many programs we have.

Source: Robin Axness, Director of Marketing and Development, Silvermine Guild Arts Center, New Canaan, CT. Phone (203) 966-9700. E-mail: robinaxness@silvermineart.org. Website: www.silvermineart.org

Attention-Grabbing Events: Nonprofit Events That Draw Interest and Support to Your Cause

KEYS TO CREATING TOP-NOTCH EVENTS

Publicity and promotion are important. Effective outreach is crucial. But building consistently positive buzz around your organization's events requires ensuring that participants have the best time possible. The following suggestions will help create events that not only keep participants coming back, but also bringing their friends and acquaintances.

Host Receptions To Die For

"On the whole, I'd rather be in Philadelphia" was the epitaph of W.C. Fields, but it may easily reflect the feelings of your supporters regarding routine receptions.

Since such gatherings are usually hosted by the organization rather than funded by ticket sales, some guests may not expect more than a few sugar cookies and coffee in Styrofoam cups, followed by a speech or two. They may even opt to stay home.

How can you use your creativity to host an event that all of your supporters will not want to miss? If it's an annual gathering, how can you make those who missed this year want to mark their calendars far in advance the next time?

Gather some of your best volunteer hosts and hostesses to brainstorm and expand on some of these ideas when you plan your next reception:

1. **Start with an attractive invitation.** Whether handwritten or printed, use attractive color and paper, or include an artistic stamp to reflect the theme or scheme. List all committee names or board member names so that those you invite will get a feeling for who will be attending. You may even say, "The board of directors cordially invites you to attend... ." Use descriptive words such as "cocktails and hors d'oeuvres buffet" or "delicious refreshments will be served" to draw more interest.

2. **Strive for quality rather than quantity.** Even if you don't wish to exclude anyone who wants to attend, send out fewer invitations than you think you need to give an aura of exclusivity. However, note in the invitation text that guests are welcome.

3. **Create an intimate atmosphere.** The most famous hostesses know that seating can make or break a party. You can use the same principles at your reception even if place cards are too formal. Use smaller tables, round if possible, to encourage conversation. Add a votive candle at each, dim the lights and play appropriate music in the background (not too loudly). String some holiday lights in large plants or as part of your simple decorations. White ones will work throughout the year.

4. **Feature a local or regional celebrity.** Even if that person won't be speaking, he or she may be happy to be your drawing card because of the good cause you support. Invite the media if appropriate, and put advance news releases in your paper to inform the entire community.

5. **Have entertainment.** A string quartet, a jazz trio or even a youth choir add a festive feeling to every gathering. If children are performing, a good contingency of parents and grandparents are certain to attend the event.

6. **Be sure food and beverages are plentiful.** Even if your budget is limited, buy or make the best food you can afford. Make refreshments easily accessible and in two or three locations so guests don't feel pressured to rush to enjoy their favorite foods before they are gone. If funds are limited, ask local bakeries, delicatessens or caterers to donate their best recipes in exchange for discreet advertising. The pace of the whole event will be more relaxed and leisurely when refreshments are plentiful.

7. **Use waiters and waitresses.** Teen volunteers may dress in attractive costumes and serve food and beverages. Make good use of those who are actors or singers, encouraging them to perform and interact with guests.

8. **Pay attention to small but meaningful touches.** Offer each lady a flower and gentlemen a boutonniere, or some small token that will make them feel special when they arrive, or as they leave.

9. **Take many photographs.** Even if those faces you snap won't be likely to see the photo later, taking lots of pictures will provide good historical background for your archives, and you can make a scrapbook or wall displays of one year's event for the viewing pleasure of those attending in future years.

10. **Keep the positive buzz going with follow-up efforts.** Create an online photo album with pictures from the reception, both posed and candid. Encourage interaction by allowing people to post comments with the photos (that you prescreen to keep them appropriate). As soon as next year's date is set, send out a Mark Your Calendar! card and encourage attendees to share the date with friends.

KEYS TO CREATING TOP-NOTCH EVENTS

Pre-Event Supports Nonprofit's Ongoing Efforts

In an effort to support the biggest fundraiser of the year for the Greater Illinois Alzheimer's Association Chapter (Chicago, IL), staff and supporters host a warm-up event. For the past two years, that event has been Purple-tini, a volunteer-hosted fundraiser that benefits the association's programs and services.

An event splashed in purple — the Alzheimer's Association's theme color — Purple-tini offers a fun-loving, relaxed mingling atmosphere for professionals. The ambiance includes specialty martinis, drinks, appetizers and dueling pianos.

Two volunteers spend six months planning details of this pre-event. Tickets are sold at $30 each to the intimate affair that typically attracts 40 to 50 guests on a Saturday evening.

The 2009 event raised $3,500, which will support the organization's largest fundraiser — the Naperville Memory Walk.

Teresa Gruber, manager of special events for the chapter, shares tips from her top volunteer and event organizer, Cathy Rittmueller, for hosting a pre-event fundraiser similar to the Purple-tini:

✓ Ask, ask, ask for money. It never hurts to ask.

✓ Work with your network of friends for help. For Purple-tini, the organization brings in the talents of a friend who works in sales at a local printing company and a friend who owns the bar that is used as the venue.

✓ Schedule the event for a time convenient for professionals to attend. Starting too early on a workday eliminates a lot of people who would likely attend otherwise.

✓ Make it a fun, relaxed event and be sure hosts mingle with guests.

✓ Be passionate about the cause. Even small pre-events involve work, and it can get discouraging when people don't respond to your invitation. Be sure not to take that lack of response personally and to always keep the end goal in mind.

Source: Teresa Gruber, Manager-Special Events, Alzheimer's Association-Greater Illinois Chapter, Chicago, IL. Phone (847) 933-2413. E-mail: teresa.gruber@alz.org. Website: www.alzheimers-illinois.org

Make Humor the Center Attraction for Your Special Event

Nothing gets people on your side — or the side of your cause — more than giving them a reason to smile and laugh.

For nine years, humor has taken center stage at Roast-a-Doc, the primary annual event for Sutter Davis Hospital Foundation (Davis, CA).

Roast-a-Doc has become a much-anticipated event throughout the region, says Kristine Stanfill, director of development at the foundation. The event is dubbed "stimulating entertainment with fiery wit " where, each year, a doctor from the organization is selected to be the focus of a roast in the name of good fun and to raise needed funds for the hospital by way of ticket sales and an auction held at the event.

Content not available in this edition

Changing things up a bit this year, two doctors — Dr. Arfan Din and Dr. Kraig Katzenmeyer — were featured in March 2010 to receive the brunt of the good-natured jokes from colleagues, friends and family. The two doctors were selected to be roasted as a team as they are frequently seen together at the hospital.

"The roast is a fantastic event in that it incorporates community members, physicians, staff, grateful patients and volunteers," Stanfill says. "We deliver an event that generates funds as well as builds lasting relationships and we have an opportunity to honor our mission publicly — a win-win on all levels."

Follow these tips for hosting a successful roast event at your organization:

• Use messaging that is simple, yet recognizable. By designing a distinct logo for this special annual event, recipients of invitations and other communications about the event instantly identify with the logo and know the communication piece is about the Roast-a-Doc event.

• Work with an independent event coordinator team. Roast-a-Doc event organizers hire two local independent event planners who plan the bulk of the event. Using independent event planners allows for more flexibility and using local planners helps the event to draw more local sponsors to support the event.

• Invite the guest of honor to select where the proceeds from the evening will be allocated. In return for being a good sport as the focus of the roast, the medical professional who is the object of the roast determines which area of the hospital will benefit from the proceeds and enthusiastically engages in the outcome and success of the event.

Source: Kristine Stanfill, Director of Development, Sutter Davis Hospital Foundation, Davis, CA. Phone (530) 750-5220. E-mail: StanfilK@sutterhealth.org. Website: www.sutterdavis.org

KEYS TO CREATING TOP-NOTCH EVENTS

Organize and Host Effective Rummage Sales

Hosting a rummage sale or tag sale as your next fundraiser can serve two important purposes: allows your organization to clean house of items that are cluttering your workspaces and raises significant amounts of money for your important cause.

Follow these tips to create a successful garage sale:

✓ **Ask your staff, volunteers, supporters and community to contribute gently used items toward the cause.** Place posters on local bulletin boards, put notices in your mailings, newsletters and on your website, call local radio talk shows and find other ways to spread the word.

✓ **Communicate what you will accept, and what you will not, for donations.** To avoid being a dumping ground, be selective on what you accept in donations and spell out this criteria in posters and other communications regarding the event. Work with your local municipality to get a dumpster donated to clear away those unsellable items and for clean up after the event. Connect with a local organization such as Goodwill to be on hand to collect items you do not wish to sell but that may be appropriate for their venue.

✓ **Sort like items.** Create areas for adult clothing, children's clothing, crafts, toys, small machinery, kitchen appliances, etc. Display items in an organized manner and be sure all are tagged with a clear and fair price.

✓ **Assign a cleaning crew to spruce up donated items and evaluate item functionality.** If an item no longer runs, for example a lawn mower, disclose this on the tag, set a low price and state that the item will be good for parts or is a fixer-upper.

✓ **Chat up your organization to garage sale attendees.** Explain that you're raising funds for a specific cause and share details. Knowing the event is for fundraising purposes will discourage attendees from bartering on price.

✓ **Have a large jar at the checkout area for donations.** Allow attendees to donate their change to promote your

---

Use Tag Sale to Showcase Cause, Seek Donations, Attract Volunteers

One simple way to create awareness of your organization at a rummage sale is to dedicate one table to spotlighting your cause.

Use that space to feature a poster board of photos showing clients receiving services, outlining how your funds are used and identifying areas in need of additional funding.

Have logo items such as coffee mugs, polo shirts or umbrellas available for a small donation (especially if you are looking to clean out your organization's closet of some T-shirts, water bottles or other items left over from a special event).

Finally, have a staff member and a volunteer or two assigned to this table to chat with passersby and turn this event into an educational community outreach as well as a way to raise funds.

---

fundraising efforts. Don't underestimate the giving nature of your garage sale patrons.

✓ **Host your community garage sale at an easily accessible area with plenty of parking and set-up space.** Consider a local grocery store parking lot, college campus or other open-air venue to allow for more space and more items for sale.

✓ **Have a cleanup plan.** Ask area students to help clean up after the event. This is where the dumpster will come in handy. Sort out items that would be useful to your local Goodwill and send a crew to make that delivery. Toss everything else.

✓ **Communicate the amount raised to all participants and attendees.** Use some of your proceeds to place a local ad in the newspaper to thank everyone for the success, announce the amount raised for your organization and, if known, announce the date for next year's sale.

Engage Young Audience With Texting Contest

Get teens and young adults involved in your cause with a cell-phone texting contest.

Whether included in a large event as additional entertainment or offered as a stand-alone event in which you ask sponsors to contribute pizza, soda and prizes, a contest that challenges the younger crowd to prove their texting mettle will get people talking.

Here's how to do it: Have a judge with a cell phone in hand. Gather participants around a table or on a stage with phones and thumbs at the ready. Have them enter the judge's

cell phone number and open their cell phone to the texting screen.

Then flip up a cue card containing the message they need to send, and shout "Go!"

The first person to send a letter-perfect text message to the judge's phone wins!

To add to the fun, limit participants to 16 people, have them face off one to one to win the best two out of three challenges, and track the winners in a Sweet 16 chart.

KEYS TO CREATING TOP-NOTCH EVENTS

Snag a Celebrity Chef to Raise the Bar on Your Special Event

Add a celebrity chef to your next event to add personality and style.

Whether the chef signs copies of a newly released cookbook, entertains guests by preparing a meal or simply mingles with the crowd, asking a chef to attend your next event will offer a fresh approach and draw more guests and media interest.

Depending on the size and scope of your event, the definition of celebrity chef could mean Food Network celebrity Bobby Flay or the chef at your area's most popular home-owned restaurant known for his/her delicious cuisine and impeccable quality.

When considering whether to add a celebrity chef to your event:

1. **Determine how the guest chef will participate.** Choose a book signing, meal preparation demonstration or an educational speech on a specific topic such as fine wines.

2. **Select a chef accustomed to public speaking,** with a large (not pompous), warm and friendly personality and who can engage an audience. If possible, see the chef in action at another event to determine if the choice is right for your event.

3. **Determine the length of time the guest chef will be at the event.** Most celebrity chefs will be at your event for one to two hours, so plan accordingly.

4. **Discuss with your guest chef how much interaction he/she will have with the event attendees.** If the chef will mingle with the guests at the event, have a staff person shadow the chef throughout the event to be on hand to assist with any needs of your celebrity chef and to answer questions about your organization.

5. **Run with the chef theme.** Attach invitations to wooden spoons or whisks, use tall chef's hats as table centerpieces, have inexpensive food-theme giveaways such as oven mitts, cookware or cookbooks — and of course, excellent cuisine.

Sites to Shop for a Celebrity Chef

Check out these websites for tips and services in booking celebrity chefs:

- Lester and Associates Event Production and Management — www.thefinestevents.com
- Chef-2-Chef — www.chef2chef.net/rank/chefs.shtml
- All American Talent — www.allamericanspeakers.com
- NoPac Talent — www.nopactalent.com

First Annual Event Puts the 'Fun' in Fun Day

The 1st annual Kawasaki Disease Fun Day raised more than $13,000 toward its $25,000 goal before the event even took place.

KD Fun Day was created to support a diagnostic test identifying the disease at the University of California San Diego Disease Research Center (La Jolla, CA). The event, along with supporting donations and sponsors, had raised $25,900, before summer events occurred. Held May 8, 2010, the fun day took place at the Stagecoach Community Park (Carlsbad, CA). Persons paid $10 admission.

Organizers of the fun day share tips to put a similar event in place:

- Create a whimsical flyer that will attract your target audience. See the flyer used by this organization to get a feel for the color, design and content by going to this link: http://www.kdfunday.org/kd/flyer.cfm.
- Have a popular teen celebrity act as master of ceremonies.

During the Kawasaki Disease Fun Day teen celebrity, Jonah Bobo, entertained guests throughout the day.

- Offer family-friendly events such as face painting, balloon animals, music and performances, professional photography, plus drawings and giveaways.
- Find event sponsors that are family- and children-oriented such as rental companies that offer bounce houses, family-friendly restaurants and children's entertainment.
- Choose a wide-open outdoor venue. Stagecoach Community Park offered a vast outdoor location that includes a children's play area and ample restroom facilities.

Source: Nicole Hershman-Daniels, Membership Event Founder & Chair, Kawasaki Disease Fun Day, Oceanside, CA. Phone (760) 433-1469. E-mail: dashnlefty@gmail.com. Website: www.kdfunday.org

KEYS TO CREATING TOP-NOTCH EVENTS

Checklist Helps Organize Show-stopping Open House

If you're planning an open house, go the extra mile to create an event that has your community buzzing for weeks to come. This checklist will help you do so.

In the months and weeks leading up to your event:

❑ Organize a planning committee and assign an event chair to oversee all planning for the open house.

❑ Recruit volunteers to assist the planning committee.

❑ Schedule regular meetings with volunteers and the committee to evaluate progress. A first task may be deciding on a theme that speaks to your mission while opening doors to possible guest speakers, decorations and giveaways.

❑ Together with volunteers and planning committee members, create a schedule with deadlines for each step of planning the open house.

❑ Prepare a media plan for publicizing your event, including who is assigned with completing specific tasks. Consider giving the media a behind-the-scenes look several days before the event to generate community buzz.

❑ Write copy for all printed materials.

❑ Distribute a schedule of events to each committee member and volunteer. Address any questions.

❑ Create an event program that includes a map, event schedule and names of people who can answer questions.

On the day of your open house:

❑ Plan for several registration tables.

❑ Have staff on hand wearing name tags indicating they are there to help.

❑ Provide refreshments, beverages and light background music.

❑ Stagger tours during the open house to prevent disruption of flow and to eliminate possible backups.

❑ Take photos to post at your website.

❑ Thank guests for coming and give them a small token such as a pen or mug to remember your organization.

Reassemble your committee and volunteers several days after the event to say thanks and to review what went well and where to improve for future events.

Enliven Celebrations With Talent Competitions

Invigorate anniversaries, reunions and other celebrations with talent competitions.

The sesquicentennial celebration for Lincoln University (Lincoln University, PA) in 2004 included student talent competitions to increase interest among students, says Sam W. Pressley, creative director, Sam W. Pressley Communications (Williamstown, NJ).

Pressley, currently consulting strategic communications coordinator for the university, was its director of marketing and communications at the time of the 150th anniversary celebration.

Under the leadership of President Ivory V. Nelson, the competitions were also created to educate students about their historic university and its significant role in higher education, Pressley says.

They promoted the competitions with campus flyers, in the campus newspaper and though in-class mentions.

An 11-member sesquicentennial commission, made up of faculty members, developed the talent competitions that included five categories: essay, oratorical, performing arts, poetry and visual arts.

"Each contest was coordinated by a faculty member who was also a commission member and served as the main contact to applicants," says Pressley.

Hundreds of students submitted applications, using forms accessible on the university's website. Students were asked to include basic contact information including student ID number and class year, and which category they were entering. Pressley says all applications were reviewed by the commission and after thoughtful discussion winners in each category were chosen by a vote.

Winners in each category were announced at the campus celebration in April 2004 that coincided with the university's annual honors convocation, which recognizes its top academic students. Winners were also announced in the student newspaper and on the student affairs and academic affairs websites. Awards and cash prizes were granted to three winners in each category: First place received $1,000, second place, $500 and third place, $250.

Source: Sam W. Pressley, Creative Director, Sam W. Pressley Communications, Williamstown, NJ. Phone (856) 582-3836.

Attention-Grabbing Events: Nonprofit Events That Draw Interest and Support to Your Cause

ONLINE, VIRTUAL AND ELECTRONIC TOOLS

The success of real-world events has increasingly come to depend on online initiatives and decisions. Whether you are looking to enhance a familiar event, extend its geographic reach beyond your immediate vicinity or replace it with a virtual option, the following strategies offer a wealth of ideas and examples.

Twitter-driven Event Draws Crowd in 15 Days

Pulling off the first-ever HoHoTO (Toronto, Ontario, Canada) event — a party at Toronto's Mod Club in support of the community's food bank — was no small feat.

In just 15 days, the Toronto technology community generated enough interest for the event to raise $25,000 for the Daily Bread Food Bank, solely by using their connections and marketing the event via Twitter (www.twitter.com). The event is pronounced hoe-hoe-TEE-oh, in recognition of the holiday season and Toronto's nickname, T.O.

Co-organizer Michael O'Connor Clarke offers tips for making a Twitter-generated event more of a success:

A single tweet probably won't do it.

"That's not how Twitter works. For ideas to take off on Twitter, you need a network effect to happen — the idea has to spread organically, picking up traction and repetitions along the way. For this, either the idea must be highly compelling and impactful, or you need a lot of people to get behind the idea."

You can't create network effects overnight.

"No organization should expect to be able to jump into Twitter (or other social media channels) and immediately see benefits. It takes time to build a community of followers, friends and interested parties who will help you to get the word out when you have something to say. Start now — if you're not already active on Twitter: you should be. If you don't get it (and a lot of people just don't — that's OK) then hire someone who does."

Spend a lot of time listening.

"Before you engage with a Twitter audience, you need to understand who they are, what they're talking about, what they're interested in, who they follow, what motivates them, what they dislike. There are lots of monitoring services and search engines you can use to do your research before you dive in. The thing is: Social media is about conversation. These conversations are multi-faceted, bidirectional and already happening. If you just jump into a conversation that's already going on without spending the time to listen to what's being said, you're only going to annoy people and your efforts will backfire."

Think through policies and processes.

"Once you engage online, you're going to find fans and critics. Nonprofit groups know they can polarize audience opinions quickly. So be prepared. What will you do when someone starts criticizing you online? How will you handle attacks? Will you respond? How do you deal with well-intentioned but off-message fans? This is a complex area — seek out a consultant who has done this kind of work for other nonprofits or organizations and ask for their help. It will be worth it."

Offer something of value.

"The incentive with HoHoTO was to have a great holiday party and be able to do some good at the same time. We created something of meaningful value for the community, and they rewarded us by showing up and giving very generously for the Daily Bread Food Bank. Simply tweeting about your great cause is not enough to really sustain people's interest — even the most charitable of us are still a little self-centered. With so many demands on our time and our pocketbooks, there has to be something valuable and worthwhile to make people want to really engage."

Source: Michael O'Connor Clarke, Vice President, Thornley Fallis Communications, HoHoTO, Toronto, Ontario, Canada. Phone (416) 471-8664. E-mail: mocc@thornleyfallis.com

Fundraising Video Connects Supporters to Their Cause

Every April the Mercer Island Schools Foundation (Mercer Island, WA) hosts its Community & Business Leaders Breakfast.

Less than an hour after it begins, the event is over and the foundation has raised almost a half-million dollars, thanks in large part to specially produced videos featuring students, teachers and foundation-funded programs.

"With the brevity of the fundraiser, we really have to touch people in a powerful and meaningful way," says Penny Yantis, executive director of the foundation. "The videos create that heart-and-soul emotional pull more effectively than almost anything else we could program."

Foundation officials produce one video a year. A four-person committee working directly with a professional videographer sets the film's theme and focus.

Yantis says the $7,000 cost to produce each video is well worth it.

"Emotional impact is what draws people in, and this allows us to tell our story in a very compelling way," she says. "The films really connect community leaders to the people and programs they would be supporting."

Check out the videos at http://mercerislandschoolsfoundation.com/impact.

Source: Penny Yantis, Executive Director, Mercer Island Schools Foundation, Mercer Island, WA. Phone (206) 275-2550. E-mail: payantis@hotmail.com

ONLINE, VIRTUAL AND ELECTRONIC TOOLS

Encourage Current, Potential Members With Online Video Tour

Go one step beyond the typical online tour of still photos and offer a video tour that grabs the attention of current and potential members alike.

The website for the Pony Express National Museum (Saint Joseph, MO) has featured a two-minute video tour since the fall of 2007. Narrated by the Cindy Sue Daffron, director of development, the video highlights different facets of the museum. A local television station that the museum regularly advertises with filmed and produced the video free of charge and also aired it on local TV as part of its monthly spotlight segment.

"The video allowed tour groups and members to see the progress in the museum and join in the progress of the museum going forward to 2010," when the museum celebrated the 150th anniversary of the Pony Express, says Daffron.

She says there was no additional cost to have the video created beyond their normal monthly advertising fee for their television spots. The video is currently available via a link on the museum's homepage.

For the first-ever video tour for the museum, the TV crew spent several hours filming at the museum, including interviewing Daffron on camera, taking pictures of the museum displays and filming visitors in the gift shop. In addition, Daffron asked the television crew to film day-camp children and others throughout the museum. Daffron was given the opportunity to view the video throughout the production process.

The video tells the story of the museum, touching on historical information, points of interest and its most popular features, says Daffron, who adds: "I have met several people who visited the site and then decided to visit the museum after watching the video."

While the museum staff has not formally tracked how many persons were inspired to become members after viewing the video tour, the director of development says she and her staff believe the video has had an impact on motivating people to join.

View the Pony Express National Museum's online tour at: www.ponyexpress.org

The video is also a beneficial tool for current members who are unable to visit as frequently as they would like, she adds, as it allows them to stay connected and reminds them how vital their support is to the museum's continued success.

Daffron says that while they currently do not track how many website visitors are viewing the online video tour, this would be a worthwhile feature to add.

She recommends that member organizations considering adding such an online feature reach out to local television stations to ask about policies and rates for nonprofits, as well as talk to members who may be able to assist in creating and producing a video.

Source: Cindy Sue Daffron, Director of Development, Pony Express National Museum, Saint Joseph, MO. Phone (816) 279-5059. Website: www.ponyexpress.org

Virtual Walkers Extend Event Reach

Your fundraising walk is a big day. But it's just one day — and what about the hundreds of people who can't make it on that day? Or the ones, who could have made the date, but live too far away?

Virtual walkers are the answer, says Jennifer Matrazzo, associate executive director of Prevent Child Abuse New York (PCANY), Albany, NY. "Virtual walkers can still raise money towards the event without having to actually be there," Matrazzo says. "The idea is really just another way to expand the scope of our walk and give people a reason to become fundraisers for us."

Walkers register through the organization's website as virtual walkers. Like actual walkers, virtual walkers are directed to firstgiving.com, where they can create their own personalized fundraising page. PCANY pays Firstgiving an annual fee for providing this service.

Another outside vendor, Democracy in Action (Washington, D.C.), handles event registration, e-mail marketing, contact management and other Web-based functions for a monthly fee, based on the number of supporters in PCANY's database.

"We were already using both of these vendors for other events," says Matrazzo, "so there wasn't any additional cost associated with adding virtual walkers. We were just finding a new use for technology and services we already had at our disposal."

This is the organization's first year of offering walkers this option. Matrazzo says the response so far has been light, but she is hopeful. "As we continue to promote the concept through e-mail and other channels, I'm hoping it will pick up. As with most events, the challenge is getting people involved. I'm hoping that a combination of persistence and creativity will result in an increased response."

Source: Jennifer Matrazzo, Associate Executive Director, Prevent Child Abuse New York, Albany, NY. Phone (518) 445-1273. E-mail: jmatrazzo@preventchildabuseny.org

ONLINE, VIRTUAL AND ELECTRONIC TOOLS

Photo Tour Showcases New Addition

Spotlight your new or enhanced facility with an online photo tour like the one used by Covenant Hospice (Pensacola, FL) to promote a building addition.

"Warm brownies, birthday parties, family gatherings, and places for family to bond are all unexpected sites at the residence," says Don Ruth, director of communications. To encourage persons to make in-person visits and experience the site firsthand, Ruth says, they promoted an online photo tour showcasing the facility's warm, inviting atmosphere.

During the addition's construction, Melissa Chapman, multimedia specialist, conducted two 30-minute photo shoots to document the progress and collect images for the photo tour. She utilized the photo album features built into the hospice's content management system, called Tendenci, to create the tour.

"Because we are a nonprofit, it was not feasible to purchase video equipment or hardware to create professional panoramic tours," says Chapman. "With basic photography equipment and Web tools, we are able to update patients, families, donors and the community as to the progress of our new addition in ways that a written description can't convey."

They notified donors by direct mail about the addition and invited them to take the online and in-person tours.

Chapman cites one unexpected perk of the online feature: Persons attending open houses "were excited to be able to go back home and show additional family members what they got to see" by logging on to the online photo tour.

Sources: Don Ruth, Director of Communications; Melissa Chapman, Multimedia Specialist; Covenant Hospice, Pensacola, FL. Phone (850) 433-2155.

Photo Contest Engages Constituents, Introduces New Mascot

Looking to promote your brand, engage your constituents and generate buzz? Host a photo contest in which your mascot or other highly recognizable icon takes center stage.

That's the tactic taken by the public relations team at Roanoke College (Salem, VA) when the college launched a new mascot — Rooney, a maroon-tailed hawk.

In the first-ever Little Rooney Spring Break Photo Contest, students were encouraged to take Little Rooney (a plush doll of the college's new mascot) on their spring break travels and photograph his adventures, says Teresa Gereaux, director of public relations. Students could submit the images for a chance to win a bookstore gift card.

"We literally laughed out loud when we saw some of the pictures," Gereaux says. "Rooney underwater. Rooney with Donald Duck. Rooney sending a hello squawk into outer space from a telescope in Puerto Rico. It was just funny and silly, and the perfect way to increase visibility of our new mascot."

Gereaux says three goals drove the contest: 1) to promote awareness of and interaction with the new mascot; 2) to enable students, faculty and staff to create content that would tie in to Roanoke's brand; and 3) to generate excitement and word of mouth.

They announced the contest to the student body by e-mail, on the college blog, and in the campus bookstore with posters and displays. They posted submissions to Facebook (www.facebook.com) as they were received.

Gereaux says winning images were not only creative and humorous, they also showed the student body's spring break activities — from a Habitat for Humanity project in New Orleans and volunteer work in Nicaragua, to skiing on the slopes of Vermont and deep-sea diving in St. Croix.

"We always try to communicate some of the interesting things our students are doing over spring break, whether it's in a blog post or something like that," Gereaux says. "This was a little bit different way, a more fun way, to do that and also accomplish some of our larger goals."

Source: Teresa Gereaux, Director of Public Relations, Roanoke College, Salem, VA. Phone (540) 375-2282. E-mail: gereaux@roanoke.edu. Website: www.roanoke.edu

Submissions to the 2010 Little Rooney Spring Break contest included Little Rooney taking to the slopes at Vermont's Mount Snow, top, and Rooney eating at Cafe du Monde in New Orleans, LA. For more examples of how Roanoke College students and faculty shared their spring break with the new mascot, go to http://roanoke.edu/About_Roanoke/Traditions/Rooney.htm and click on the link Little Rooney Photo Contest.

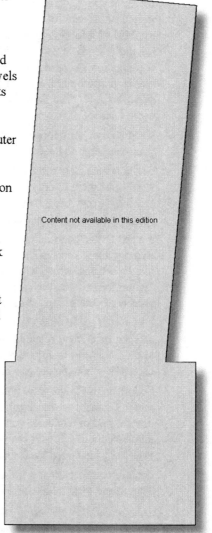

Content not available in this edition

ONLINE, VIRTUAL AND ELECTRONIC TOOLS

Twitter-based Fundraiser Brings in $10,000 in 10 Days

Nonprofit organizations across the country have had varying degrees of success in harnessing the power of Twitter networking to bring in much-needed donations. Through these groups' trial and error, a best-practices approach is emerging that can help you decide whether a Twitter-based fundraiser will work for you.

One successful group has been the ChristmasFuture Foundation (Calgary, Alberta, Canada), a Canadian-based nonprofit that funds projects worldwide to help erase extreme poverty. ChristmasFuture raised more than $10,000 in the 10 days before Christmas 2008 with its TweetmasFuture fundraiser, says operations manager Leif Baradoy. In all, it brought in about 7 percent of the group's annual budget.

"We've only really been around for two years as an organization, but the key to our success was that we have been able to powerfully represent ourselves through our projects," which include everything from youth arts and leadership programs in Nicaragua to funding a water sanitation project in Sierra Leone, Baradoy says.

The TweetmasFuture campaign didn't have a lot of planning involved, Baradoy says, but it did require a way to donate money online. They sent direct messages on Twitter to many of their 400-plus followers, asking them to donate and/or send out tweets (brief messages sent to subscribers through Twitter) about the campaign. All they had to do then was keep the word going.

Here are Baradoy's tips for a successful Twitter fundraiser:

✓ Invest in your followers: Those who have successfully raised thousands of dollars from Twitter activity all have something in common, Baradoy says — they have established a following on the social networking site for at least a year, and regularly send out useful updates (like articles, blog posts, etc., that relate to the organization's core mission) to engage their supporters in conversation. In other words, if you build trust with your social network, you build potential for a larger donation pool. "People will only share links and donate if they are convinced it is a good cause," he says.

✓ Keep it short: Any longer than 10 days is too long, Baradoy says. You don't want your campaign to become noise in the background.

✓ Give persons clear direction. In your initial message, state exactly what you would like them to do, which is basically to donate and retweet, Baradoy says. Don't try to say too much, as tweets are limited to 140 characters.

✓ Create a fundraiser Web page: The fundraiser should have its own Web page, and the link to that page should be included in every message you send for the event, Baradoy says. You can shorten the link through the use of computer applications like Tweetdeck, which will also help you keep track of your followers. Include your Twitter feed on that Web page, as well as publicity and links to other important aspects of your group. Make it easy for people to navigate and, of course, to donate.

✓ Use a hash tag to track the campaign: Hash tags allow Twitter users to search for all specific content related to that tag, so including one in each message related to the fundraiser is important if you want to see who's supporting you. Baradoy used #TweetmasFuture as a hash tag, but planned to shorten it for the 2009 effort.

✓ Follow up: Keep the word going by tweeting about how much money has been raised. Chances are those will be passed on, as well. Publicly thank those who have donated and/or retweeted your messages by sending a reply on Twitter. Consistent involvement in a Twitter campaign is fundamental to success, Baradoy says.

✓ Don't just take, give back: ChristmasFuture bought some of its own online donation gift certificates and sent them to the most involved Twitter followers. They could make a donation in their name or pass the gift along to a friend.

Contact: Leif Baradoy, Operations Manager, ChristmasFuture Foundation, Calgary, Alberta, Canada. Phone (866) 629-0516. E-mail info@christmasfuture.org

---

Tweeting For a Cause

Here are some sample "tweets" sent through www.twitter.com from the many staff and supporters of the ChristmasFuture Foundation (Calgary, Alberta, Canada) during a social network-driven fundraising effort in December 2008:

Kinghuang: Check out TweetmasFuture, ChristmasFuture's campaign to help end extreme poverty! http://www.christmasfuture....
4:10 PM Dec 16th, 2008 from Twitterrific

RT @UniversalGiving: Let's get this rolling! Get involved & spread the word about raising money for #tweetmasfuture http://twurl.cc/9yu
4:22 PM Dec 17th, 2008 from TweetDeck

#tweetmasfuture goal status: $3577 of $20,000 . I WEEK LEFT. http://bit.ly/3aDvSZ
8:30 PM Dec 18th, 2008 from TweetDeck

Cool fact: #tweetmasfuture has increased traffic to the site by +29% since Dec. 16th. Help spread the word about http://bit.ly/3aDvSZ
4:26 PM Dec 19th, 2008 from TweetDeck

Want to give www.christmasfuture.org a try? Go to the site, hit Receive & enter this code: eawlyyemtzep . First to use it gets it! *11:56 AM Dec 23rd, 2008 from TweetDeck*

Status: $16,082 of $20,000 for TweetmasFuture. Help push it over the edge and give someone an innovative gift http://bit.ly/rnnS
10:13 AM Dec 24th, 2008 from TweetDeck

One final tweet. We are $2500 away from our goal. Give a gift that helps end poverty at http://bit.ly/rnnS
3:35 PM Dec 24th, 2008 from TweetDeck